Sistergirls
@ work

Sistergirls @ work

A Devotional

CAROL M. MACKEY

Published by Revell
a division of Baker Publishing Group
P.O. Box 6287, Grand Rapids, MI 49516-6287
www.revellbooks.com

Spire edition published 2013

ISBN 978-0-8007-8830-8

Previously published under the title *Sistergirl Devotions*

Printed in the United States of America

13 14 15 16 17 18 19 7 6 5 4 3 2 1

This book is dedicated to my mother-in-law, Beulah Mackey, and to all of the Lord's hardworking daughters.

Contents

Acknowledgments 11

Introduction 13

1. Use What You Got to Get What You Want: *Make the Most of Your Opportunities at Work* 17
2. Timeliness Is Next to Godliness: *Show Up to Work On Time Every Day* 20
3. What's in a Name? *Establishing Your Identity at Work* 22
4. Some People Are Never Satisfied: *Beware of the Chronic Complainers* 24
5. Write It Down: *Putting Your Goals on Paper Is the Key to Achieving Them* 26
6. The Waiting Game: *How to Cultivate Patience While You Wait on God* 28
7. The Sheep and the Goats: *Which One Are You?* 30
8. Commit . . . or Quit: *Stop Being Mediocre and Exceed Your Reach* 32
9. Community Outreach on the Job: *You Are Jesus's Helping Hands at Work* 35
10. A Blessing in Disguise: *How to Use a "Bad Boss" Experience to Your Benefit* 37
11. Jesus Loves the Little Children . . . but Not at Your Desk! *Use Wisdom if You Have to Bring Your Kids to Work* 40
12. Get Up, Stand Up: *Standing Up for What's Right* 42
13. Why Can't We Be Friends? *Making the Transition from Friend to Boss* 44
14. On-the-Job Training: *Exploring the Pit Stops along the Way* 46
15. Develop an Attitude of Gratitude: *In All Things, Give Thanks* 48
16. "It's Not My Fault": *Own Up to Your Mistakes* 50
17. Service First: *How to Serve Your Way to Greatness* 52
18. Fly with the Eagles or Cluck with the Chickens: *You Decide* 54

19. Temper, Temper: *Why You Must Keep Your Cool* 56
20. The New You: *Don't Let an Old Lifestyle Hold You Hostage* 58
21. "Did You Ask?" *Boldly Make Your Needs Known* 60
22. Don't Talk about It, Be about It: *Let Your Actions Speak Louder than Your Words* 62
23. We Fall Down . . . but We Get Up: *How to Bounce Back after a Setback* 64
24. Dress to Impress, Not Distress: *What Do Your Clothes Say about You?* 66
25. He's Got Your Back: *God Is in Total Control, No Matter What* 69
26. Sister Power! *Thank the Lord for Godly Sisters* 72
27. Daughter, Where Art Thou? *God Never Turns His Back on Us* 74
28. Family First: *Your #1 Ministry* 77
29. God Has a Plan for Your Life: *Don't Second-Guess Yourself* 79
30. Through the Fire: *How to Come through Hardship as Pure Gold* 81
31. Signs and Wonders: *Believe in Miracles for Yourself and Your Co-workers* 84
32. Sleep on It: *Don't Make Hasty Decisions When You're Angry* 87
33. Lord, What Am I Doing Here? *You're Exactly Where You're Supposed to Be* 89
34. Use It or Lose It: *Why Your Daily Devotions Are Important* 91
35. Avon Calling? *When to Keep Your Outside Interests Away from the Workplace* 93
36. "Put Some Weight on the Bar": *Exercise Your Faith and Strengthen Your Spirit* 95
37. "Don't Even Go There!" *Keep Your Mind Free from Negativity* 98
38. Get Over It: *Let Go of Past Mistakes and Missteps* 100
39. Gossip Girls: *Staying Away from Toxic Co-workers* 103
40. Take a Load Off: *Find Time for Yourself Every Day* 106
41. Returning to Work: *Making the Transition from Home to Office* 108
42. Girl, Watch Your Mouth! *Positive Confession Equals Positive Results* 111
43. Love in the Afternoon: *Use Discretion When Dating a Co-worker* 114
44. Dream On: *Make Your Vision a Reality* 116
45. Gone Fishin': *How to Really Win Souls* 119

46. Don't Be Hatin': *There Are Enough Blessings to Go Around* 122
47. The Value of Work: *God Will Supply All Your Needs* 124
48. Pray without Ceasing: *Keep Your Communication Lines Open with the Lord* 126
49. What Is Your Vision? *Know Where You're Going So You'll Know How to Get There* 129
50. Develop a Giving Spirit: *Opening the Door for Great Blessing* 131
51. When Racism Rears Its Ugly Head: *Confronting Painful Situations with Grace* 134
52. Father Knows Best: *When God Says No* 136
53. A Prophet without Honor: *Family and Friends May Doubt You, but God Never Does* 138
54. Exceed Your Reach: *Go the Extra Mile and Experience Greater Blessings* 140
55. On-the-Job Moms: *Fostering Independence in Your Kids* 142
56. Never Remain Neutral: *Take a Stand and Stick to It* 145
57. Keep It Real: *Showing Your Vulnerability Will Strengthen Your Witness* 147
58. Just Do It: *Waiting and Procrastinating Aren't the Same Thing* 149
59. Sexual Harassment on the Job: *Adopt a Zero-Tolerance Policy for Workplace Abuse* 151
60. Deciding to Stay Home with Your Kids: *Banish the Guilt and Embrace the Blessing* 154
61. Turn Your Back on the Crowd: *Focus on Your Goals and Leave the Naysayers Behind* 156
62. Go Ye! *Discipleship Is Key On the Job and Off* 159
63. Build Bridges, Not Walls: *Finding Kindred Spirits* 161
64. Let Me Upgrade You! *God Wants to Promote You and Elevate You to New Heights* 163
65. Let Go and Let God: *Don't Let Unforgiveness Block Your Blessings* 166
66. When Work, Church, and Home Collide: *How to Manage Conflicts and Set Priorities* 168
67. Know When It's Time to Go: *If You've Outgrown Your Position, God Will Move You On* 170
68. My Soul Says Yes: *How to Develop a Willing Spirit* 172
69. Wise Counsel: *Why Mentors Are Important at Every Level* 175
70. How a Shepherd Leads: *Managing People Is Never Easy* 178

71. Ready When You Are! *The Lord Is Ready to Bless You—Are You Ready to Receive?* 180
72. Get in the Mix: *Polish Your Networking Skills* 182
73. Get a Life: *All Work and No Play Will Make You a Lonely Girl* 184
74. Starting Out and Starting Over: *Embrace New Beginnings* 186
75. "I'm Only a ___________": *Don't Let Titles Limit You* 189
76. Fearfully and Wonderfully Made: *Celebrate Being a Daughter of the King* 191
77. Fridays and Mondays: *Don't Abuse Sick Days* 193
78. All Change Is Not Bad: *Embrace the Positives That Change Brings* 195
79. Develop a Spirit of Excellence: *Expect the Best from Yourself and Others* 197
80. All Working Mothers Are Managers: *Use Your Job Skills to Keep Things Cool at Home* 199
81. Save for a Rainy Day: *Get a Savings Plan—You Never Know What May Come Up* 201
82. Keeping Peace at Home: *Make Time for Your Mate* 203
83. An End May Be Just the Beginning: *Layoffs and Letdowns Can Be a Hidden Blessing* 205
84. Name It, Claim It, Do It! *Put Action behind Your Words to See Results* 207
85. Lord, I Need a Miracle! *When Things Look Hopeless, God Shows Up and Shows Out!* 209
86. More Territory: *Watch God Multiply Your Talents and Gifts* 211
87. Tough Decisions: *What Would Jesus Do?* 213
88. Pursue Your Passion: *Work at Your Dream While Working Your Nine to Five* 216
89. How to Love the Job You Hate: *Other Things May Not Change, So You Have To* 218
90. The Lord Giveth and the Lord Taketh Away: *Remain Humble as You Achieve Success* 221

Acknowledgments

To my Lord and Savior Jesus Christ: in you I live and move and have my being. There's no greater love.

To my family, Jerry Sr., Jerry Jr., and David Mackey. Thank you so much for your love, understanding, and patience while I wrote and wrote and wrote. It was as much of a new experience for me as it was for you. I appreciate your support and love you guys more than you know. Big Jerry, thank you for giving up not one but two vacations so I could get this book done. Now that I've got my life back . . . Martha's Vineyard and South Beach, here we come!

To my mom and dad, who instilled in me a tireless work ethic and refused to let me make excuses for being black, being poor, or being a girl. Dad, though you never graduated from high school, you always stressed the importance of an education, and I'll always remember your words: "What's in your head, can't nobody take away." Mom, thanks for the old-school Southern wisdom—it's brought me a mighty long way.

To my siblings, for their love and support, but especially to my sisters Brenda Campbell and Joyce V. Williams, who have cheered me on in every promotion, commendation, and award I've received throughout my career.

To the Mackey family: thanks for the love and prayers over the years. To my father-in-law, Larry Mackey Sr.: thank you for showing me that tough love never goes out of style. And to my mother-in-law, Beulah Mackey, to whom this book is dedicated: I finally heeded your advice (or rather, order!) to "write that book!"

To Minister Denise J. Brown, sistergirl extraordinaire, prayer partner, and the best attorney a girl could have. You've been a huge blessing to me, and I know God is working in and through you.

To my editor, Andrea Doering: you've been a great friend, a great boss, and a great editor. Your insight, encouragement, and prayers got me through the toughest days. Thank you so much for believing in me and for being obedient to the Holy Spirit. You're a mighty woman of God. And a special thank you to Baker Publishing Group, especially Jessica Miles, Michele Misiak, Nathan Henrion, and the fabulous Max Eerdmans. I appreciate your patience while this newbie author learned the ropes!

To my mentors, Terrie M. Williams, Henry McGee, and Brigitte Weeks. All three of you are very different, but the common denominator is your selflessness. I've learned so much from each one of you, and you've been shining examples of what mentors should be. "Thank you" is an understatement.

To Pat Lomax: you embody the true meaning of a friend. As a fellow writer, you were understanding and patient while I was writing this book, and that is appreciated more than you know. To my other sistergirls whom I love dearly: Dianne Mackey, Maria Conforti, Karen Hunter, Kim Givens, Yvette Hayward, Nancey Flowers, Janet Hill-Talbert, and Mondella Jones. Thank you all for the love and support you show me over and over again.

To Bishop J. Raymond Mackey, my very first pastor. Thank you for stressing the importance of being rooted and grounded in the Word. All of my spiritual "firsts" occurred while I was part of your ministry, and for that you'll always be special.

Introduction

When I first became a Christian, I envied people who worked in Christian organizations and businesses. They got to live their faith openly on their nine-to-five jobs. I'd listen like a wide-eyed child as they talked about how they'd begin each day with corporate prayer and have lunch-hour Bible study fellowships. I then wondered, *What about me, Lord?* Little did I know that over the years, God would take me on a spiritual journey I'd never forget. And the mission field I was assigned to was my own place of employment.

I wasn't an evangelist or a prophet or a teacher or a preacher. I didn't have any of those titles, nor did I covet them. Yes, I held minor positions in church, but nothing that required active ministry. I was a wife, a mother, and a church-going believer who loved the Lord, and that was a ministry in itself. But as I grew in Christ, the Holy Spirit showed me that God's not interested in our titles; he's interested in us. I learned that it doesn't matter if you labor on the mission field in Communist China or if you wait tables at the local IHOP or if you're the CEO of a Fortune 500 company—you're equally as important to God. And he wants to use you to build his kingdom.

The Great Commission is to go out and "make disciples of all nations" (Matt. 28:19). God didn't put a disclaimer on that command. He didn't say you had to have a college degree, sing in the choir, or have model looks. This word is not only for pastors, teachers, preachers, and evangelists. It's also for you and me. It's for every believer in Christ Jesus. And your workplace is fertile ground. No matter where you work—a deli, the hospital, or a major corporation—God has called you to be salt and light wherever you are and whatever you do. God isn't hung up on titles. He's looking for a few good men (and in our case, women) who will shine Christ's light in a dark world.

Although my walk hasn't been perfect, being a Christian has helped me get through the toughest of times, especially on the job. And I'm here to tell you that if God did it for me, he'll do it for you too, for God doesn't show favoritism (Acts 10:34). I've seen God's hand move mightily on my behalf on so many occasions that I sit and marvel at his goodness, his mercy, and his grace. Have I made mistakes? Yes. But each mistake resulted in knowledge and wisdom I couldn't have gotten if I'd paid for it. Makeup pioneer Mary Kay Ash said, "We fail forward." There will be bumps in the road—at home, at church, and on the job. Conflict is inevitable. But with the Lord's help, you can be successful at whatever you undertake.

If God can't do something, it can't be done. He can break the chains of racism. He can soften the heart of a tyrannical boss. He can "find" money for you when there's no money to be found. If you do your part (faith and obedience to his Word), he will do his (bless you abundantly). God is faithful to the end. He wants our light to shine so that men will see our good works and give him glory (Matt. 5:16). It's up to us to exercise our faith and to become willing vessels.

I don't profess to be a Bible scholar or a human resources expert. But what I'd like to help you see in these pages is that 1) God loves you more than you can imagine, 2) he wants to use you for his glory on your job, and 3) you don't have to be a "perfect" Christian; you just have to be willing and available. You don't have to be famous or have a college degree or speak eloquently to be used by God.

Although we can respect and admire those in active ministry, God's blessing isn't limited to those with titles. I'm not in full-time ministry, but I've still had the privilege and the honor of being a vessel for the Lord Jesus Christ in the workplace. I've led folks to Christ, prayed for the sick and seen them healed, and watched as my own heart's desires were manifested right before my very eyes—experiences I will never forget. But it wasn't about me; it was how the Lord worked in and through me. I'm not special. I just made myself available. That's it. God did the rest.

I hope you will find comfort, support, encouragement, ideas, and hope within these pages. I wrote them just for you—from one sistergirl to another. Now you, my sister, go out into the world and make our Father proud!

Peace and blessings,
Carol M. Mackey
November 2009

1

Use What You Got to Get What You Want

Make the Most of Your Opportunities at Work

The LORD said to him, "What is that in your hand?"

EXODUS 4:2

I always loved watching *The Ten Commandments* on TV every Easter Sunday when I was a child. My family would be huddled around our tiny black-and-white set, waiting for Moses's big feat: to part the Red Sea and escape the angry Egyptians in hot pursuit of God's people. I became a Christian some twenty years later, but that scene was my first introduction to God's divine power. I discovered how it signifies not only unwavering faith but also that God will use whatever you have to help you attain your goals. All Moses had was a large stick, but God used this ordinary item to get extraordinary and miraculous results.

My first job out of college was hardly what I expected. Although I was fresh out of college and armed with a BA in communications, the large salary with the corner office I'd imagined somehow evaded me. Instead, I ended up answering phones at the reception desk in one of the most successful ad agencies in New York City. I loved the quirky creative types (I felt they were kindred spirits since I too was a writer), the dressed-to-the-nines account executives, the celebrity clients who wandered in and out for meetings, and the carefree and fun environment each day provided.

Sure, my Colgate smile and sweet demeanor were a boon at the agency, and mine was the first face clients and visitors would see. I was well liked. But I wanted in. I wanted to show the bigwigs that I brought more to the table than just a cheery telephone greeting. I was willing to work hard if they gave me a shot.

The next step for me was an administrative assistant position. The only thing stopping me was a typing test that I could not pass. The human resources manager told me I just needed to take a typing class and practice typing as much as possible. I felt defeated. Here I was with a college degree and couldn't get a better-paying job because I couldn't type fast enough.

But all that changed when my boss transferred me to the reception desk on the fifth floor. I was a little bummed about it, because the fourth floor was the one always bustling with activity, and the CEO and president were there, so at least I got face time with them. But God works in mysterious ways. The first day I went to my new desk upstairs, I saw the answer to my unspoken prayer: a brand-new electric typewriter, with a typing book to boot! I hadn't asked for a typewriter—or a typing book—but God knew the desires of my heart.

When the desk was slow, I'd volunteer to type envelopes, letters, or anything else that others had for me. I needed the practice and they needed the help, so it worked out. A few months later, I became the secretary to the president and to the vice president of a subsidiary of the agency. The Lord opened the door for me, and I was able to use what was available to take my career to the next level.

What do you have in your hand?

POWER MOVE

There are opportunities and resources all around. In these cost-conscious times, many companies have either eliminated or cut back on training, so free classes or lectures may not be an option. However, for a nominal fee many community colleges offer one-day seminars and weekend programs tailored to your career path. Take advantage of every opportunity for on-the-job growth, tuition reimbursement, one-on-one mentoring with senior managers, or lunchtime seminars. The more you know, the more you grow.

MY CONFESSION

I will make use of all the resources God provides to help me reach my goals.

2

Timeliness Is Next to Godliness

Show Up to Work On Time Every Day

Obey with enthusiasm, as though
serving the Lord and not people.

EPHESIANS 6:7 NET

I admit it. I'm not a morning person and never have been. According to my mother, I was a "night owl" in utero—wide awake, kicking until the wee hours of the morning (I guess I tired myself out). The poor woman couldn't even get a good night's sleep *before* I was born, let alone after. And to this day, I get my second wind around four p.m. When everyone else is winding down their workday, finishing up what's left on their to-do lists, I'm just getting started—tackling big projects that I know will carry over well into the evening, long after everyone's gone home.

I've had problems in the past getting to work by nine o'clock. When I was a struggling single mother, my newborn would keep me up all night, and I'd be dog-tired the next day after only three hours of sleep. At the time, I was a receptionist and had to open the doors for the staff and visitors, so it was imperative that I was prompt. One of the best things about advancing in my career was getting more flexibility on when I showed up!

Jesus admonished us in Matthew 22:21, "Give to Caesar what is Caesar's, and to God what is God's." Your company has probably mandated certain work hours for you, and it is your responsibility to adhere to that schedule. "Caesar" (your employer) expects you to render the hours you committed to when you were hired. So make it your business to be on time.

Say you're up for promotion. You have all the credentials on paper—your annual reviews are great, you go over and above your normal duties, you're friendly and well liked—but you're habitually late. It could ruin your chances for the promotion. So ask yourself: If Jesus were your boss, would you drift in late every day? Would you give him "attitude" if he mentioned your tardiness or threatened to write you up if it continued? Of course you wouldn't. Ephesians 6:7 invokes us to be obedient to our employers and to diligently work as if the Lord himself were our boss—because ultimately, he is.

POWER MOVE

Try to come into work a little early at times. Even fifteen minutes makes a difference if you're vying for a promotion or a raise. Employers want to know that you are reliable and dependable. Most senior managers start their days very early, so if you want face time with them, get in well before regular hours start and the office gets busy.

MY CONFESSION

I will be prompt and honor the hours my employer has set for me, for Jesus is my ultimate boss.

3

What's in a Name?

Establishing Your Identity at Work

A good name is more desirable than great riches;
to be esteemed is better than silver or gold.

PROVERBS 22:1

When I was a teenager in the late seventies, rap music was a fledgling art form. Many of the songs were about women—lighthearted and sometimes funny stories that ran the gamut from failed relationships to tributes to hardworking black mothers. But none of the lyrics I recall put women in such a derogatory and shameful light as they do today. Now so many media outlets refer to women as the b-word that weary censors have even given the word their stamp of approval. It causes me to wonder: does society have so little respect for women that it's now okay to call them names? I once heard a spoken-word poet say, "It's not what you're called, but what you answer to," and I couldn't agree more. What name do you answer to?

Lazy. Arrogant. Unapproachable. These are just a few of the negative labels that can be put on a woman in the workplace. If you refuse to do someone else's job, you're lazy. If you dare to voice your opinions with conviction, you're arrogant. If you're naturally shy and introverted, you're unapproachable. Whether this may be true of your situation or not, labels stick. The saying "sticks and stones may break my bones, but names will never hurt me" is untrue. That's why your character must always outweigh any name anyone assigns to you. The Pharisees were always on Jesus's case, seeking to destroy him and refusing to acknowledge that he was the Son of God. However, despite their most diligent efforts to discredit him among the people, these leaders could find no sin in him.

Sometimes you will come against harsh criticism for a decision you've made or a belief you hold dear. You may be called names that are not fitting of you, but you must keep your integrity intact, for "the LORD abhors those who are perverse in heart, but those who are blameless in their ways are his delight" (Prov. 11:20 NET). The choice is yours: which name will you answer to?

POWER MOVE

Words have power, so refuse to accept any negative name that someone gives you. If the criticism is coming from a trusted friend, it should be received with love. Ask the person why he or she feels that way, and really listen. None of us is perfect, and there's always room for improvement.

MY CONFESSION

My good name is priceless, and I refuse to let anyone place negative labels on me.

4

Some People Are Never Satisfied

Beware of the Chronic Complainers

Do everything without complaining or arguing, so that you may become blameless and pure, children of God without fault.

Philippians 2:14–15

There's one in every office. The co-worker who never stops complaining. The person who will put a damper on everything, regardless of the good going on in others' lives. You get a promotion and they warn you about "selling out." You get a raise and they tell you how much more you'll have to pay in taxes. You get engaged and they point out the high divorce rate. Though they may be a very dedicated worker and even a good friend, a dark cloud hangs over them because they always find something to complain about. They never see the glass as half full or count their many blessings.

Don't get me wrong, there are times when we all complain about one thing or another—from triple-digit heat in August to our husband refusing to pick up his socks (again) to being overcharged at the dry cleaner. Life is full of both good and bad moments, but I'm talking about people who don't see the good in anything—or anyone.

What do you do when these ungrateful folks bring their misery to your doorstep? Lay the Word on 'em. Quote Scripture: "You know, God's Word tells us that 'pleasant words are a honeycomb, sweet to the soul and healing to the bones'" (Prov. 16:24). If the people are Christians, they will be convicted by the Holy Spirit (and hopefully healed). If they're not believers, I predict one of two things will happen: either they will not come around you anymore because they think you're crazy, or they too will be convicted and will want to hear more (Heb. 4:12). At the very least, they will have been exposed to God's Word. And just think of how much Scripture you will have committed to memory! So it's a win-win situation.

POWER MOVE

Pray for the complaining brother or sister who refuses to see God's many blessings in their lives and always points out the negative. Continue to set an example and be the light Christ wants you to be in a dark world. Give thanks in all things and see God's goodness and grace in every life experience. If all else fails, break company with these folks. Cut your phone calls short, and make yourself unavailable for social gatherings. They'll get the hint. Some people are toxic, and no matter what you do, you can't change them. But you can change your association with them.

MY CONFESSION

I will count my blessings and give thanks to God even during the dark times in my life. I will encourage others to focus on the positives in life as well.

5

Write It Down

Putting Your Goals on Paper Is the Key to Achieving Them

> And the Lord answered me, and said, Write the vision, and make it plain upon tables, that he may run that readeth it. For the vision is yet for an appointed time, but at the end it shall speak, and not lie: though it tarry, wait for it; because it will surely come, it will not tarry.
>
> Habakkuk 2:2–3 KJV

A tangible testament of God's commandments was so important to him that he entrusted Moses to be keeper of it and to deliver the message on the tablets to the people of Israel. God could have easily told Moses to commit the Ten Commandments to memory, but he knew a written record would last longer and be an everlasting reminder of his faithfulness to future generations. So he inscribed those blocks of stone with the words the Israelites were to live by. And the same holds true today. Just as our words have power when spoken, they have power when written down as well. In order to obtain success, we must write our goals down.

What do you want? A promotion? A new house? A better marriage? Then write it down. It's been said that people who write down their goals achieve them faster than those who don't. Apparently, there is a connection between putting ideas, thoughts, goals, and dreams in writing and having them come to fruition. In some professions, written goal setting is mandatory, because companies know it works.

When I joined Weight Watchers, I was asked to set—and attain—5 and 10 percent weight-loss goals during my weight-loss journey. I was openly applauded and rewarded when I reached them—and that felt great! And no wonder: the written word has biblical roots, as evidenced in Habakkuk 2:2.

I believe that when you write down your goals, dreams, and visions, something is released in the spiritual realm. God wants to bless you abundantly as you seek his will for your life. "Delight yourself in the LORD and he will give you the desires of your heart. Commit your way to the LORD; trust in him and he will do this" (Ps. 37:4–5).

POWER MOVE

Start now! Get out a pen and paper and write down the things you want to accomplish both on the job and at home. Nothing is too small or large, so you may as well dream big. Give yourself a timetable for both short- and long-term goals, but don't get discouraged if it takes longer to meet them than you'd hoped. Keep your list in sight, review it often, and monitor your progress. Your goals will come to fruition if you have faith and stay committed to achieving them.

MY CONFESSION

As I put my goals, dreams, and desires for my life on paper, God will give me the faith, resources, and opportunities necessary to bring them to pass.

6

The Waiting Game

How to Cultivate Patience While You Wait on God

There is a time for everything, and a
season for every activity under heaven.

Ecclesiastes 3:1

"Just wait on the Lord" is the advice you've probably heard so much that it's become cliché. God our Father has ordained perfect order in everything he created. As King Solomon says in Ecclesiastes, there's a season (time) for everything. Flowers won't bloom during a snowstorm. An infant can't eat a steak. You get the idea. The truth is, God has ordained the natural order of things for our lives. Like it or not, *we must wait our turn*. We must also realize that nothing is outside of his perfect order and perfect will for our lives. The Lord says, "For I know the plans I have for you . . . plans to prosper you and not to harm you, plans to give you hope and a future" (Jer. 29:11).

We are exactly where we are supposed to be. We may think we're ready to take a higher position. But do we know everything involved in performing this job? At times, we may think we're smarter, more educated, or better qualified for the job. And that may be true on rare occasions. It just may not be our time. We may have some more learning to do or more experience to gain. Or maybe we're just not mature enough right now to handle such a position. I don't believe God will set us up for failure. Rome wasn't built in a day, and our careers won't be either. When he has something for us, no one can take it away.

POWER MOVE

Waiting is never easy (or fun), but it's worth it. So commit yourself to the process of learning and growth and watch the opportunities arise for you. God will open doors for you that no man can close!

MY CONFESSION

I know that God has the perfect job for me. I will wait patiently on his perfect timing for my life.

7

The Sheep and the Goats

Which One Are You?

I tell you the truth, whatever you did for one of the least of these brothers of mine, you did for me.

MATTHEW 25:40

In Matthew 25:31–46, Jesus refers to two types of followers—the sheep and the goats. He outlines the differences between the two and why each will inherit either eternal life or eternal damnation. In a nutshell, the sheep go the extra mile to do the Father's will, while the goats refuse to.

In a nonbiblical context, there are some parallels that can be drawn from this example. I believe there are "sheep" and "goats" in every workplace. Sheep are team players and support the overall goals of leadership. They are big-picture people who look beyond present circumstances. Now, don't get me wrong; sheep are not passive yes-men or brownnosers. They may have a strong opinion about an issue and will voice it, but at the end of the day, they support leadership whether they agree with the company's new direction or not. They try to make the best of every situation.

Goats, on the other hand, may be labeled as difficult, and it takes a bit more convincing to get through to them. They don't adjust well to change, and some are in desperate need of an attitude adjustment. Goats tend to be more open about their displeasure and may denounce leadership for making what they think are bad choices. They stubbornly dig their heels in and may refuse to comply. They are less apt to follow and may have to be "pulled" into submission.

At the end of the day, who do you think is the most valuable to the company—the sheep or the goat?

POWER MOVE

If you've had a few jobs, I'm sure you've seen both "sheep" and "goats." You may have even been one or the other during different work situations. But the sheep will go further than the goats in any working environment. Goats have a limited time on the job because they're dispensable. So strive to be a sheep—someone who is teachable, a team player, and a good listener. You will see the difference it makes in your work life.

MY CONFESSION

I purpose to become a "sheep," someone who is leadable and teachable.

8

Commit . . . or Quit

Stop Being Mediocre and Exceed Your Reach

Lazy hands make a man poor, but
diligent hands bring wealth.

Proverbs 10:4

Merriam-Webster's Dictionary defines the word *mediocre* as "of moderate or low quality, value, ability, or performance." But I was struck about two other words next to that definition—"ordinary" and "so-so." Both of those words left a sour taste in my mouth. Who in the world would ever want to be ordinary or so-so?

God wants us, through our obedience to him, to excel, even on the job. He wants to make us the head and not the tail, the top and not the bottom (Deut. 28:13). But he can't do that if we're operating in a state of mediocrity or we're just getting by. Jesus won't stand for mediocrity at the judgment. "I know your deeds, that you are neither cold nor hot. I wish you were either one or the other! So, because you are lukewarm—neither hot nor cold—I am about to spit you out of my mouth" (Rev. 3:15–16).

In a scene from one of my favorite movies, *The Devil Wears Prada*, the main character, Andy, complains that she's not making any headway with her boss, the editor-in-chief of an iconic fashion magazine. To her surprise, Nigel, the magazine's creative director, coolly replies, "Then quit." She stammers, "But I'm trying so hard!" He laughs and tells her that she's not trying hard. As a matter of fact, she wasn't trying *at all* to be a good assistant. Throughout the movie, she snickered and made fun of the stick-thin, four-inch-heeled staff, mocked the designs, and didn't take the time to learn what her boss required. So Nigel was right. Andy didn't try because she didn't *commit.* She took the job just to get her foot in the door to a career in journalism. But when she fully committed to learning the industry, the fashions (including ditching her boring wardrobe for designer duds), and, most of all, what her boss wanted and needed, she excelled.

Granted, that's a Hollywood movie, but think about your own life. Do you feel like you're just going through the motions? Do you have an "I don't care about this stuff" attitude? Have you been passed over for promotions even though you've been on the job a long time? If you answered yes to any of these questions, think about your contribution to your job. God wants his daughters to outshine the daughters of the world: "No one lights a lamp and hides it in a jar or puts it under a bed. Instead, he puts it on a stand, so that those who come in can see the light" (Luke 8:16). The workplace is no exception.

POWER MOVE

Most companies want to promote from within, so see what you have to do to move up. Positive action is the first step. If you possess strong skills in a different area you'd rather be in, make it known and take steps to move over. Become more visible to senior management by offering to head a committee. If management offers free classes or training in a specific area, volunteer for them. This shows initiative, and your manager will see you as someone who is serious about getting ahead. Put yourself in a position to be blessed—and to be a blessing.

MY CONFESSION

I commit to learning, growing, doing, and becoming better on the job, as the Lord would want me to.

9

Community Outreach on the Job

You Are Jesus's Helping Hands at Work

Then he said to his disciples, "The harvest is plentiful but the workers are few. Ask the Lord of the harvest, therefore, to send out workers into his harvest field."

Matthew 9:37–38

The very fact that you are employed is a blessing in itself. No matter what you do or where you do it, you receive wages for the job you perform. There are some people who will never hold down a job, through no fault of their own. That's why it is our Christian duty to serve those who cannot help themselves (James 1:27). The Lord admonishes us to feed the hungry, clothe the naked, and visit the sick (Matt. 25:35–36), for "the poor you will always have with you" (Matt. 26:11).

My sister Joanie is a perfect example of this biblical principle. She has served for years in the homeless ministry in her church in Brooklyn, New York. She is the first one to solicit donations of gently worn clothes, shoes, coats, and other items from her co-workers to give to the homeless ministry.

Even with her tiny frame, she lugs bags of clothes onto the subway for the long train ride from her job to her church.

Another friend of mine donates leftover books to his church's library. Some restaurants donate leftover food to the homeless shelters throughout the city.

Jesus himself was a master recycler—remember when he fed the five thousand with the loaves and fishes? He told the disciples, "Gather the pieces that are left over. Let nothing be wasted" (John 6:12). We can learn from his wonderful example of meeting people at their point of need and not wasting resources. It doesn't matter where you work or what item you want to give, be it food, clothes, magazines, books, or any other thing that can benefit the poor or underprivileged. Do your part. You are Jesus's arms and legs on this earth.

POWER MOVE

Find some way to give to those in need and encourage your co-workers to do the same. Just about anything in good condition—clothes, shoes, books, toys, dishes—is accepted at most homeless shelters and organizations. Do you have a suit, a dress, or shoes that you don't wear anymore? Donate them to a place like Dress for Success, an organization that helps disadvantaged women reenter the workforce. The Bible says, "It is more blessed to give than to receive" (Acts 20:35), so take God at his Word—and be more blessed!

MY CONFESSION

There will always be someone less privileged than I am, so I will do my best to share with them what I have and encourage others to do the same.

10

A Blessing in Disguise

How to Use a "Bad Boss" Experience to Your Benefit

Everyone must submit himself to the governing authorities, for there is no authority except that which God has established. The authorities that exist have been established by God.

ROMANS 13:1

At some point in your working life, you will have a bad boss—or at least one you think is bad. According to Romans 13:1–5, there is no boss (governing authority or authority figure) that God has not put in place. Yes, even the bad ones.

It's easy to report to a boss who is kind, fair, understanding, and committed to your growth and development. She's the first one to give you a pat on the back and to sing your praises to her boss. She may put you in check when you need correction, but it's not with a hateful or degrading spirit.

But then there is the boss who constantly undermines you, is not supportive, and is always on you for the slightest infraction. It may not seem right or fair, and you may feel like, "Lord, why me?" I believe God in his sovereignty has a reason for you to be reporting to that person at that time.

The Lord makes no mistakes; you are exactly where you are supposed to be. There may be an important lesson you have to learn that only this person can teach you—and it may be totally unrelated to the work you do. Maybe patience is the lesson (think about that raise you're overdue for). Maybe it's perseverance (you may want to just quit). And maybe it's just so you can be a witness to that boss.

It's my belief that people who like to make others' lives miserable are spiritually bankrupt. Their lives are so joyless and unfulfilled that they use their jobs as a substitute to satisfy the emptiness. When they see that a job cannot fill that spiritual void, they take their frustration out on you. You may be the light that illuminates their darkness or demonstrates the love of Christ in ways they cannot fathom.

Most of all, pray without ceasing (1 Thess. 5:17). Some of my biggest battles have been won through prayer. I've seen the most arrogant and stubborn person transformed by the power of the Holy Spirit. Now, this is not to say that you should be demeaned, degraded, or abused at work. If a boss is misusing you or violating your civil rights as an employee, go to your human resources manager to correct it. The Lord certainly doesn't want his children abused or misused. But a tremendous blessing can come out of a bad situation at work through prayer and perseverance. You just have to recognize that God is in every detail of your life—even the ones that make you uncomfortable.

POWER MOVE

Make every effort to see your boss through Christ's eyes. The Lord has you in your job for a reason, so be willing to trust him to lead you, guide you, and direct you regarding your boss. Let your light shine (Matt. 5:16), be obedient to God's Word (even when you're ready to slap someone!), and see the salvation and power of God work in your life (Isa. 1:19).

MY CONFESSION

Even though it may be difficult, I will love the unlovable, just as Jesus did. I will pray for and bless my boss. I will embrace the learning experience and look forward to the blessing I will receive.

11

Jesus Loves the Little Children . . . but Not at Your Desk!

Use Wisdom if You Have to Bring Your Kids to Work

In everything set them an example
by doing what is good.

Titus 2:7

If you're juggling parenthood and a job outside the home, you know that sometimes child care can be dicey. The kids may be out on holiday break, school may be closed for a snow day, day camp may be over, or your babysitter may be sick. Whatever the circumstance, you may be fresh out of options and have no choice but to bring your child to work with you. What do you do? What would the Lord want you to do?

Unless it's "Take Your Child to Work" day, bringing your child to work should probably be a last resort. Some companies are more lenient about children in the workplace, while others will not tolerate it at all. You should be sensitive to your boss's leading on the subject. If you work in an open environment or outdoors, bringing your child to work may be dangerous and strictly forbidden for insurance reasons. If you work in an office with a looser policy, and depending on the age of your child and the nature of your business, bringing him or her to work may be just fine.

School-age children may be able to sit quietly in their parents' area, reading or coloring. Your teen may even serve in an intern capacity—photocopying documents, filing, or doing other clerical tasks. But preschoolers with short attention spans bore easily and may run through the hallways, throw temper tantrums, or become unruly during the course of the day. They are children, after all, and must express themselves.

Will your child's presence interfere with your job function? After all, you're Mommy to them, and they will demand your attention. If their presence disrupts your workday and disturbs your co-workers, it's probably better to take a personal day and stay home with your child.

Your office is a place of business and not a day-care center, so use wisdom when deciding to bring your child into the office. Your first ministry is to your family, so now is the time to create a backup plan. Ask God's help in coming up with plans that won't leave your child in an unsafe or unhealthy environment or jeopardize your livelihood.

POWER MOVE

When child-care plans fall through, it can be a stressful time for you and your child if you don't have a backup. Check with your boss first to see if he or she is cool with your child being at work. If you get a mixed or negative reaction, don't do it. Take a personal or vacation day and stay home with your child.

MY CONFESSION

I will use wisdom—both practical and godly—when it comes to blending my home life and my work life. I know the Lord will guide me in my decisions regarding my children and their care while I'm at work.

12

Get Up, Stand Up

Standing Up for What's Right

I know that the LORD secures justice for the poor and upholds the cause of the needy.

PSALM 140:12

Some of us get incensed at injustice. Whether it's the assistant who's uncomfortable with a boss who stands a bit too close or the executive who constantly belittles her staff in front of other employees, seeing inappropriateness in the workplace makes your blood boil.

It's okay to get angry about ungodliness and wrongdoing. Remember, Jesus turned over all the tables when he saw the people buying and selling in the synagogue. He said to them, "It is written, . . . 'My house will be a house of prayer,' but you have made it 'a den of robbers'" (Luke 19:46). Just as God's house isn't the place for gambling or soliciting, the workplace was not meant for foolishness or wrongdoing. If you're truly concerned about the welfare of your co-workers, you're a good listener, and people respect your opinions, you should consider representing your fellow employees by hearing their grievances and taking them to upper management. Someone needs to fight on their behalf, and it may just have to be you!

POWER MOVE

Are you a hearer or a doer of the Word? It's easier to complain about an issue than to do something to tackle it. If you feel led by the Spirit to represent your co-workers on the job, then go for it. Not only will you be defending the rights of your co-workers, but you'll also be presenting the needs of others to senior management. Let your light shine!

MY CONFESSION

I will stand up for my own rights and the rights of others on my job.

13

Why Can't We Be Friends?

Making the Transition from Friend to Boss

Many curry favor with a ruler, and everyone
is the friend of a man who gives gifts.

Proverbs 19:6

You were once friends with a co-worker—going to lunch every day, sharing confidences, hanging out during nonworking hours. This friend knows your true feelings, your aspirations, and your goals. In other words, she knows where the bodies are buried. So what happens when you get a long-awaited and well-deserved promotion . . . and you're now *her* boss? How do you handle the friendship?

Use the Lord's example. Although he handpicked the Twelve and technically was their boss, he called himself their friend. "I no longer call you servants, because a servant does not know his master's business. Instead, I have called you friends, for everything that I learned from my Father I have made known to you" (John 15:15). You can read all of John 15 to get the full understanding of what Jesus was commanding his disciples, but the bottom line is, they knew his deity and respected it.

Similarly, if you have an employee who was once a friend (or may currently be), she must also respect your new role. As a boss, you will be privy to confidential information that you cannot share with your team. "A gossip betrays a confidence, but a trustworthy man keeps a secret" (Prov. 11:13). You will know who is up for a big raise or a promotion and who is slated to be let go. You will make unpopular decisions because you're expected to do what's best for the company, not individuals.

What if your friend tells you she just knows you're going to "hook her up" with a raise or a promotion because you're friends? If she is a hard worker, has had great reviews, and is a consistent performer, she should be rewarded. But if her work reputation is shaky, you have to deal with her expectations and be honest with her. She may not take this news lightly and may even rebel, calling you a sellout or accusing you of "thinking you're something" now that you're the boss. You may experience all kinds of backlash. But that will also let you know you didn't have a friend after all; you had a lunch buddy. For "a friend loves at all times" (Prov. 17:17) and would respect your judgment.

POWER MOVE

If you get promoted over your peers or friends, ask God for wisdom and guidance in dealing with the situation. It's a sticky one to be in, but not unique to forward-thinking go-getters who want to make a difference for Christ. You'll have to be more patient, humbler, and more selfless than ever before. Don't approach your new position with "I'm the boss now" arrogance. Godly leaders are servants first, so seek to build bridges, not walls.

MY CONFESSION

If the Lord promotes me on the job, I know he will equip me to succeed in all areas of my new role, even the more challenging ones.

14

On-the-Job Training

Exploring the Pit Stops along the Way

Your beginnings will seem humble, so
prosperous will your future be.

Job 8:7

At some point in our lives, we all may have to take a job that's not necessarily on our career path. We may need health benefits. We may need a regular paycheck while pursuing our dream. Or we may simply need to put food on the table. Stocking shelves at a supermarket, flipping burgers at a fast-food joint, or ringing up toothpaste and deodorant may not be your idea of climbing the ladder of success, but you can still be a blessing in whatever position you have.

Kate Wendleton, founder of the Five O'Clock Club, a job-search strategy group, defines a job as "just only a bridge" or a stepping-stone to greater things. Some jobs will be short-term and others will last longer than you expected, but know that the Lord wants to use you wherever you are. He wants you to perform just as willingly, have just as much integrity, and represent him just as well as you would if you were the president of a major corporation. Oftentimes the Lord wants to see how we handle the small things before he blesses us with bigger things. "For a man's ways are in full view of the LORD, and he examines all his paths" (Prov. 5:21).

For example, while I was grocery shopping one weekend, the cashier ringing me up greeted me with a smile, double-bagged my fragile items, thanked me, and told me to have a nice day. I could see she cared about her job, even though she was "only" a cashier earning minimum wage.

If you are a conscientious, hardworking, and diligent cashier, most likely you'll be a conscientious, hardworking, and diligent CEO. Of course, you'll get wiser as you learn and grow with each position, but your work ethic and core values will remain the same. So remember, you carry Christ with you wherever you go and in whatever you do.

POWER MOVE

If you're in an entry-level position, go over and beyond the call of duty and treat your job as if you were earning ten times the amount on your paycheck. A job can be "just only a bridge" to the abundant blessings God has in store for you. "Lazy hands make a man poor, but diligent hands bring wealth" (Prov. 10:4).

MY CONFESSION

As I serve with gladness, I know God is preparing me for bigger and better things every day.

15

Develop an Attitude of Gratitude

In All Things, Give Thanks

Give thanks in all circumstances, for this
is God's will for you in Christ Jesus.

1 Thessalonians 5:18

If you grew up like I did, you were taught to say "thank you" if someone gave you a gift or did something special for you. Even if the gift wasn't to your liking or was inexpensive, you thanked the person. My mother summed it up best: "Nobody has to do anything for you or give anything to you. So you'd better be grateful when they do." That advice has stayed with me through the years, and I've taught these principles to my sons as well.

The Lord wants us to have thankful hearts because of his grace and mercy. Being thankful opens the door for greater blessings. If we can't thank him for the small things (a parking space), how can he bless us with big things (healing from illness)?

Every year right before Thanksgiving, my company distributed $25 gift cards to employees to use at their local supermarket. The employees could either use the gift card themselves to help defray the cost of their holiday shopping, or donate it to one of the local charities. Either way, it was a nice gesture. Most people were grateful just to get the help, especially those with large families.

But then there would be folks who would complain that the participating supermarkets were miles away from their homes, or that the amount was too little, or that they would've preferred a cash bonus, not a cheap gift card. Their ingratitude was like fingernails scraping on a chalkboard. Eventually my company merged with another and the program was discontinued. And those very same people were complaining about not receiving any card that year!

We don't miss the water until the well runs dry. So be grateful for everything.

POWER MOVE

Thank God for the small things—a seat on the bus, a coupon from your favorite boutique, your sister taking the kids for the weekend so you can sleep in—and he will bless you with the big things. Gratitude opens the door for bigger and better blessings in your life.

MY CONFESSION

Lord, I thank you for all of my blessings, great and small.

16

"It's Not My Fault"

Own Up to Your Mistakes

The one who covers his transgressions will
not prosper, but whoever confesses them
and forsakes them will find mercy.

PROVERBS 28:13 NET

Mistakes. Bloopers. Faux pas. Boo-boos. Mea culpas. Whatever we choose to call them, errors are bound to happen, especially on the job. The good news is, everyone has made them and will continue to make them—from the CEO on down to the lowest-level employee.

In the Garden of Eden, when God asked Adam if he'd eaten from the tree of the knowledge of good and evil, Adam admitted that he had, but not without blaming Eve. "Yes, but it was that woman's idea" (see Gen. 3:12). And Eve was no better. She blamed the serpent (Gen. 3:13). Adam and Eve both made a mistake—and sinned against God—but neither one took responsibility for it. Although no one likes to make mistakes, we will get more respect from others if we own up to them.

I remember early in my career at a newspaper, before the world of email, I sent out a memo in which I basically blamed myself and our department for a mistake we'd made. Letter writing was my forte, so the tone of the memo was succinct and apologetic for the error. I CC'd my bosses, as I always do, and put the memo in the interoffice mail slot. The minute it hit my director's inbox, I was summoned by her assistant. I knew I was in trouble. Both she and my manager looked at me as if they'd seen a ghost.

"You can't be serious," the director said, while my manager stared at me, armed crossed.

"I'm sorry . . . serious about what?" I asked innocently.

She waved the memo at me. "Carol, you took blame for this and made us all look like idiots."

I didn't see it that way and told her so. I was simply telling the truth. It *was* our fault. She shook her head and told me to intercept the mail and to retrieve the memo immediately. I did, and it never arrived at its intended destination.

If you've made a mistake and done all in your power to rectify a problem, there's nothing else you can do. So don't beat yourself up about it. This too will pass!

POWER MOVE

It's an old cliché, but honesty really is the best policy when it comes to admitting to errors on the job. Yet beware: corporate environments can be snake pits, so use godly wisdom and judgment as to what you own up to. Be firm about which mistakes were your fault and which ones were not.

MY CONFESSION

When I make mistakes, I will own up to them and learn from them.

17

Service First

How to Serve Your Way to Greatness

The greatest among you will be your servant.
MATTHEW 23:11

Jesus is the perfect example of a servant. He was constantly drumming this message into his disciples while he was still on earth: to really be great, they had to have a servant's heart. Service—not servitude—is an asset, especially in the workplace. And it's not limited to those in customer-service positions. I'm talking about true service—unselfishly putting the needs of others ahead of our own.

Some people are just naturally nurturing and will instinctively lend a helping hand in times of need. They don't care about titles, monetary status, or social standing. They just see a need and fill it. You've probably seen co-workers who are always giving their time and energy to others—getting lunch for a pregnant co-worker whose feet are swollen or volunteering their lunch hour to teach a new employee a complicated database. They always help when they can.

But service is not a sign of weakness. Just imagine if Jesus "shut down" after a few miracles. What if he copped an attitude when Mary and Martha asked him to visit their brother

Lazarus when he was sick? Or if he didn't want to be bothered when the woman subject to bleeding desired only to touch the hem of his garment for her healing (Mark 5)? So many people's lives would have been different had the Lord not given of himself so freely. Was he tired in some of those instances? Absolutely. He was human, after all. But he was also divine, and that part of him desired to see people healed, delivered, and set free. Jesus still gave of himself completely and tirelessly. We are to follow his example.

POWER MOVE

If you really think about it, there has probably been a time when you could have given more of yourself but didn't. We've all been there. But it's not too late. Opportunities for service are all around, and you can contribute even in the smallest way. So offer to pitch in. If your work is slow and you see your boss is frazzled, offer to take something off her desk. She'll appreciate your initiative and the much-needed help. My former assistant Diane would do this all the time, and I loved her for it. Little things mean a lot!

MY CONFESSION

As I follow Jesus's example, I will seek out ways to become a better servant as the Holy Spirit leads. When I serve others, I serve him.

18

Fly with the Eagles or Cluck with the Chickens

You Decide

They that wait upon the LORD shall renew their strength; they shall mount up with wings as eagles; they shall run, and not be weary; and they shall walk, and not faint.

ISAIAH 40:31 KJV

Years ago, a minister visited our church, and the topic of his sermon was "Eagle Christians." The members of the congregation had puzzled looks on their faces. "Eagle Christians—what are those?" one woman whispered. (An older member who was hard of hearing thought he'd said "Evil Christians," and we chuckled at the oxymoron.) His sermon compared strong Christians with the most powerful birds in the animal kingdom—eagles. We can learn a lot from eagles and apply those characteristics on the job.

Eagles don't simply fly; they soar, and they can reach altitudes of ten thousand feet or more. The eagle's motto might be, "The sky is the limit!" Chickens, however, are a heavy-bodied bird and can fly only a few feet off the ground.

Perhaps that's why they often wind up on someone's dinner table by nightfall!

Eagles' heads are held high. Chickens, on the other hand, have to bend over and peck their way through life for survival, pushing other chickens out of their way to eat and drink. (This is where the term "pecking order" comes from.) Is it any wonder that rap artists call disrespectful women "chicken heads"?

Eagles are faithful and committed—they mate for life. Chickens are polygamous—ten to twelve hens to one rooster—when they choose to mate. Eagles are team players. While nesting, the male and female eagles share responsibility for their young, taking turns sitting on the eggs and nurturing the fledglings.

Notice that the Bible rarely mentions chickens, but eagles are mentioned on several occasions. Two very different birds with two very different mind-sets—one is very focused and committed, the other is selfish and limited. So which would you rather be—an eagle or a chicken?

POWER MOVE

Refuse to buddy up with unhappy co-workers who just want to cluck and stay on the ground year after year. The Lord wants you to "mount up with wings as eagles" and soar. He has given you all the tools you need to succeed. It's up to you to make the choice: either soar through the sky with the eagles, or stay on the ground with the chickens.

MY CONFESSION

Like the eagle, I will be strong and determined.

19

Temper, Temper

Why You Must Keep Your Cool

A fool gives full vent to his anger, but a
wise man keeps himself under control.

PROVERBS 29:11

Let's face it—we are a passionate people. Just visit any black church across America. It's one of the things that other groups admire, and it's what makes us uniquely "us." Passion is like a two-edged sword, though. Passion toward a worthy goal or cause can be a blessing. But paired with anger, it can be lethal. That's why it's crucial that we keep our negative feelings at bay when things go wrong on the job—even when we're 100 percent right.

Whether we're being passed up for the promotion we worked so hard for all year, or whether a co-worker threw us "under the bus" in front of our boss, we have to maintain our calm. That's not to say we should be a doormat and not speak up for ourselves. It simply means we have to remain in control—no yelling, cussing, or threatening to harm someone. Ephesians 4:26 reminds us not to sin in our anger, for God knows that anger and sin go hand in hand.

We are human, after all, but let's remember Jesus's example when we feel like we're going to lose it. Jesus was belittled, degraded, insulted, mocked, and scorned, but he always remained calm and in control. The only time in the Bible he showed his anger by getting physical was when men were in the temple buying and selling. Jesus "overturned the tables of the money changers" (Matt. 21:12), stating, "'My house will be called a house of prayer,' but you are making it 'a den of robbers'" (v. 13). In the Old Testament, God got angry (Exod. 22:24; 2 Kings 22:13; Ps. 95:10). But his anger is righteous anger. Because of our sinful nature, our anger is often anything but righteous—we get mad and want to bust some heads! But we have to remember whom we serve and represent.

POWER MOVE

Like it or not, you are being looked at, even when you think you aren't. Society has perpetuated certain stereotypes about black people, especially black women—and if we even raise our voices, it can be misconstrued as belligerence. So when people get on your last nerve, take a deep breath, say a prayer, and remember you represent Christ. This is your place of business, and your career and livelihood could be threatened if you act out. If you have been wronged or insulted by someone, take a few hours (I wait a day), then tell them your feelings. Most likely they will apologize or at the very least acknowledge your feelings. If they don't, bless them, turn them over to God, and let him deal with their hard hearts.

MY CONFESSION

No matter how angry I get or how many people have wronged me on my job, I will first pray and ask God to give me a greater portion of self-control. He is my avenger!

20

The New You

Don't Let an Old Lifestyle Hold You Hostage

One thing I do: Forgetting what is behind
and straining toward what is ahead.

PHILIPPIANS 3:13

We wouldn't be human if we didn't make mistakes. But to dwell on them won't do us any good—especially when we become unproductive and immobile. God wants us to move ahead despite our faults and shortcomings. He said he'd throw our sins "into the depths of the sea" (Micah 7:19).

Sometimes people want to remind you of who you used to be—a drug addict, an ex-con, even something like being known as the girl who always has an excuse or does only half the job. When people look down on you, remember, "All have sinned and fall short of the glory of God" (Rom. 3:23), so don't worry about your past life. Everyone has one. Once you commit your life to Christ, you are a new creation. "If any man be in Christ, he is a new creature: old things are passed away; behold, all things are become new" (2 Cor. 5:17 KJV). This is especially true when you're trying to reacclimatize into society if you were incarcerated or in a rehab center. You want to make a new start, but folks want to constantly put you down when you're trying to do what's right. It's easy to get discouraged, but you must turn a deaf ear to their criticisms. Remember, your God is a restorer and doesn't want you to wallow in the past.

Just think of the apostle Paul. Who was more vehemently opposed to Christianity and new converts of Christ than he, a devout Jew? Yet after his conversion experience, he was more devoted to the cause of Christ and salvation than anyone. No one would have guessed that this man had actively persecuted Christians.

As God used Paul to preach the gospel, Paul's sordid past was soon forgotten. In fact, he was the one who reminded new believers of the man he used to be—and how Christ had changed his hard heart. Paul had a hateful past but a godly testimony.

POWER MOVE

During moments of self-pity and self-doubt, it's easy to dig up skeletons from your past. Banish those thoughts from your mind; they're coming from an ungodly perspective. As a Christian, you now have "power from on high" (Luke 24:49) and are a serious threat to the enemy. Satan wants you stuck in the past because it's the region of regret—just like his eternal home, hell. Ask for forgiveness for your mistakes, forgive yourself, and move on. You've got great things to do for God, and he needs you to carry them out. Live fully in the present so he can bring about your bright future!

MY CONFESSION

I refuse to wallow in the past but will live totally in the present as a committed servant of God. I am a new creation in Christ!

21

"Did You Ask?"

Boldly Make Your Needs Known

For everyone who asks receives; he who seeks finds; and to him who knocks, the door will be opened.

Luke 11:10

On a particularly stressful day, I had a conversation with a trusted mentor and fellow sister in Christ. I was lamenting on how my business unit never really had the manpower to flourish and be better and more profitable. I complained that a lack of staff had inhibited me from implementing the programs necessary to take my unit to the next level. I told her how almost single-handedly running new programs had burned me out, and I was beginning to feel unappreciated and resentful toward upper management.

This friend, a wise woman who had a stellar career in publishing, simply looked and me and said, "Well, did you ask?" I couldn't even muster an answer. Truth be told, I had not asked for anything, so I got nothing. Fear of being turned down had stopped me from asking for the help I so desperately needed.

If the man with leprosy had not asked (begged) Jesus to heal him, he may have still been stricken with the disease

(Mark 1:40–42). If Jairus, the synagogue leader, had not asked Jesus to come to his house to visit his dying daughter, she may have never been raised to life (Luke 8:41–42, 49–55).

What are you asking for at work? More staff? A promotion? A raise? An office? More flexible hours? Whatever it is, state your case. If you don't ask, you can't receive. Your boss is not a mind reader and cannot know what your needs are if you don't communicate them. But first pray and ask God for direction. Sometimes the things you want may not be good for you at that time. God may not be saying no; he may be saying to wait. But you'll know only if you ask!

POWER MOVE

Don't let fear of rejection stop you from asking for whatever it is you desire or feel you deserve. The worst that can happen is your boss says no. Be prayerful and thoughtful about your requests. Make sure they will benefit not only you but also the company, since your boss will probably wonder what's in it for the company. Be prepared to show your boss.

MY CONFESSION

As I go boldly to the throne of grace to make my requests known to God, I will also go boldly to my boss and ask for what I want or need. God will divinely order my steps.

22

Don't Talk about It, Be about It

Let Your Actions Speak Louder than Your Words

Do not merely listen to the word, and so deceive yourselves. Do what it says.

James 1:22

Some days it's really tempting to "talk the talk" of faith. Anyone can answer with "I'm blessed" when asked how they are. Anyone can wear a cross around their neck. But God is looking for your hands and feet, not just your mouth.

For example, say a co-worker has had a fire and lost everything, so your office takes up a collection. When the envelope hits your desk, do you tell yourself, "God will take care of them," or do you donate money or clothing? Or say the boss has asked everyone to volunteer their lunch hour to wrap gifts for the annual Toys for Tots Christmas charity. Do you stay at your desk, or do you help? Jesus commanded us to act, not just pray, if someone is in need (Matt. 25:25).

These are two small examples, but it's the little things that sometimes matter most. Most of us in general can talk a good game. But people are looking to see if we live up to what we profess. When we only play at faith, it just makes unbelievers call us "hypo-Christians" and say things such as, "That's exactly why I don't go to church." Titus 1:16 sums it up best: "They claim to know God, but by their actions they deny him."

We're not responsible for others' excuses; they will have to answer to God for them. But we are responsible for showing love, compassion, and other Christlike qualities to the world. The Lord loves for us to profess him, but he also wants our actions to line up with our talk. It's perfectly fine to be about God's business and be proud of it. But keep in mind that your actions really do speak louder than your words.

POWER MOVE

See where you can be more of a "living epistle" without saying a word (see 2 Cor. 3:1–3 KJV).

MY CONFESSION

I will be a doer of the Word and let my actions speak louder than my words.

23

We Fall Down . . . but We Get Up

How to Bounce Back after a Setback

In this world you will have trouble. But take heart! I have overcome the world.

John 16:33

When I first became a Christian, I thought all of my worldly sorrows would be over. Because I was new in the faith, I didn't know that God allows adversity in our lives so we can grow and develop in Christ. In my naïveté, I thought that any negative experience came from the devil. The truth is, sometimes it's our own fault. Bad decisions, poor judgment, ignorance, or plain old selfishness will land us in a heap of trouble. I also learned that what Satan intends for evil, God will use for good (Gen. 50:20).

The year 1993 was a bad one for our family. Our home went into foreclosure, our car was repossessed, and we were burdened financially. My husband's business folded and my salary wasn't enough to keep everything going, so we made the decision to let the house go. We had hit rock bottom, and it was a terrible feeling.

I dreaded going back to work, fearing questions about what had happened. Worse yet, because my job was so deadline-oriented, I feared not being able to concentrate.

But actually, work was a pleasant distraction—it kept my mind off what was going on at home. I wasn't given the luxury of wallowing in self-pity or woulda-coulda-shouldas. I had two little boys depending on me for support. I had to get up, get dressed, and go to work every day.

What I learned during that time is that God is bigger than even the biggest troubles. The house and car were just material things, and although we were inconvenienced and uncomfortable, we got over those losses in time. We bought another house a few years later and have had a few cars since then. But I had changed spiritually. One of the Scriptures that resonated with me during that time was Matthew 5:45: "For he maketh his sun to rise on the evil and on the good, and sendeth rain on the just and on the unjust" (KJV).

Christians aren't exempt from hardship. There's always going to be heartbreak, tragedy, or disappointment in this life. But we can take comfort in knowing that Jesus is there for us through the pain and suffering.

POWER MOVE

Just because you're down doesn't mean you're out, and best of all, it doesn't mean that your situation will last forever. If you've experienced a loss of any kind—material possessions, a relationship, or a job—know that God will be there to comfort you through the process of healing. He is a replenisher, and whatever you've lost, he can restore. It's his pleasure to bless us, and it's our job to have faith.

MY CONFESSION

My God is bigger than any setback or problem I have. I will trust him to deliver me from any painful situation.

24

Dress to Impress, Not Distress

What Do Your Clothes Say about You?

I also want women to dress modestly, with decency and propriety, not with braided hair or gold or pearls or expensive clothes, but with good deeds, appropriate for women who profess to worship God.

1 Timothy 2:9–10

Everyone takes notice when a stylish woman enters a room. Her outfit is tasteful, her hair and makeup are impeccable, and her shoes are polished and scuff-free. In other words, she's got it going on! Although the Lord wants his daughters and sons to look presentable, we have to be mindful not to overdo it. Some jobs may have a more relaxed dress code, while others, such as sales, require a wardrobe that reflects success—expensive suits and shoes, manicured nails, and expert grooming. In sales, first impressions are lasting, and presentation is vital. Though dressing to the nines in Prada and Gucci is nice, the Lord has a better wardrobe plan—to "clothe yourselves with compassion, kindness, humility, gentleness and patience" (Col. 3:12).

I'll never forget the time I wore black leather pants to work, where I was a project manager at a major newspaper. I was in my twenties and had an hourglass figure, and I remember exactly what I wore that day—butter-soft leather pants, a cashmere turtleneck sweater, and black designer pumps. But I'll also never forget the reaction I received from one of my colleagues who knew I was a Christian. Joel (not his real name), a middle-aged Jewish man, couldn't help but "admire" my outfit and fixed his gaze on my hips. "Hmm, hmm, hmm, Carol. I bet you drive those deacons crazy on Sundays when you wear those pants." Flattered (how dumb was I?), I simply smiled and said, "Oh, silly! I don't wear these to church!"

We all had a good laugh, but later that day in the cafeteria, one of my dear sisters in Christ pulled me aside. "Carol, you know, you really shouldn't wear those to work. They're pretty revealing," she said, motioning with her eyes toward my rear end. I got the picture. And I never wore them to work—or anyplace else—again. If a simple thing like wearing leather pants could change the way a co-worker looked at me, then I was willing to retire them.

Looking back, I can see that those leather pants represented my life "BC" (before Christ) of clubbing, drinking, and partying with my single girlfriends. Maybe this was the Lord's wake-up call for me to retire those pants—and their connotations—for good. I like looking my best and feel more confident when I'm well dressed.

Although God wants us to represent him well physically, I think he's more concerned about our spiritual condition. A harsh, critical spirit isn't flattering on anyone!

POWER MOVE

Wardrobe choices are always personal, but remember that when you're in a place of business you will have limitations, even in the most casual settings. Clean, pressed, and neat clothes never go out of style. Most of all, remember that you are in essence "working for the Lord" (Col. 3:23). And he's one boss you don't want to disappoint.

MY CONFESSION

I will be sure to represent the Lord well, even in my clothing choices. He is my ultimate boss.

25

He's Got Your Back

God Is in Total Control, No Matter What

Know therefore that the LORD your God
is God; he is the faithful God, keeping his
covenant of love to a thousand generations of
those who love him and keep his commands.

DEUTERONOMY 7:9

There have been times in my career when the road was rough and I felt like giving up. I remember one particular time when I was assigned yet another marketing director, after we'd had several over the years. Marge (not her real name) was one of the smartest marketers in the company and was known for boosting sales and revenue. I was pleased to be working with her and looked forward to it. For my first meeting with her, I had prepared myself with everything she would need to understand our part of the business.

When we met, I barely got through the first five minutes of my presentation when she cut me off mid-sentence and started telling me how she planned to run things. I never got through my presentation and abruptly left her office after she cut me down so quickly. I could tell this relationship would be rocky.

A few days later, one of my fellow editors pulled me aside and said, "I see Marge is your marketing director. She's not too fond of our side of the business." This colleague, a white male, went on to share his unfruitful experience with her. So now I knew her approach with editors wasn't personal—or racial.

Almost immediately, I understood what he meant. Marge came in with guns blazing, removing editorial content (my pride and joy). Soon it became a battle of wills, and one day I acted completely out of character and got into a shouting match with the woman. Who was she to tell me what my demographic (black women) wanted? I was hurt and insulted.

The human, fleshly side of me dug my heels in. I was as obstinate as she was and wasn't giving in. But in my heart, I knew it wasn't an earthly fight; it was a spiritual one. "For our struggle is not against flesh and blood, but against the rulers, against the authorities, against the powers of this dark world and against the spiritual forces of evil in the heavenly realms" (Eph. 6:12). Did I think Marge was evil? No. Was she just as passionate and strong-willed about her job as I was about mine? Absolutely!

We were two cooks in the same kitchen, and I was miserable. I loved my job and knew I was just hitting my stride career-wise, but I hated the current situation. I wished—prayed—that Marge would get transferred to another part of the company.

Then one day, something miraculous happened. The Holy Spirit softened my heart—and hers. I accepted—and even appreciated—her input and advice and recognized her true value to our business. We became more congenial toward one another, and she even invited me to lunch. We chatted over salads like old friends, and I had fun. What I found in Marge was an engaging, charismatic, and hardworking mom just like I was.

Several weeks later, Marge announced that she and her family were relocating to another state. I attended her going-away soiree and sincerely wished her well. The Lord had intervened when I needed him most and taught me a good lesson. He had never left me. He was always there, working things out for my good (Rom. 8:28).

POWER MOVE

When challenges come, sometimes it's easy to think God has forgotten about you. Just because he doesn't answer your prayers doesn't mean he isn't working on your behalf. Sometimes life has to be a little uncomfortable so you can learn something. But just know that there will be a resolution and you'll come out stronger and smarter because of it. "Let us hold unswervingly to the hope we profess, for he who promised is faithful" (Heb. 10:23).

MY CONFESSION

When the storms at work are raging, I know the Lord is with me and will deliver me from all oppressive situations. My Daddy's got my back!

26

Sister Power!

Thank the Lord for Godly Sisters

Charm is deceptive, and beauty is fleeting; but a woman who fears the Lord is to be praised.

Proverbs 31:30

Black women share a bond of sisterhood that is unmistakable, unbreakable, and unshakable. We have friends for years—from childhood through adulthood and until we see the Lord. We're sisters forever and forever sisters. But sisters in Christ are an extra blessing no matter what point in our lives we meet them—in church, at school, or in the line at the movie theater. Like recognizes like, and there are some sisters we'll instantly bond with. Because jobs can be stressful and isolating for Christian women, it's always a blessing to have other godly women praying for us, supporting us, and encouraging us in the Word.

One such sister for me was Terrie Simonson-Allen, a dear friend of my husband's family who later became my co-worker. Terrie was known for her bright and bubbly personality and sweet spirit. Everybody at the newspaper where we worked loved her, and so did I. She took me under her wing, introducing me to others who could support me at work. At the time, I didn't have my driver's license, so Terrie, who also lived in my town, would pick me up and drop me off. Often we'd stop at the supermarket on the way home and she'd wait until I picked up a few groceries. She was more than a friend; she was like family.

At work, Terrie arranged a weekly Bible fellowship every Tuesday (with management's permission), where we'd pray, read Scripture, and even sometimes have a guest speaker come in. I met several ministers who have since become good friends as a result of this fellowship. Whenever I had a grueling day at work, Terrie was always there to listen, whisper a Scripture in my ear, or pray with me. Her presence in my life was an inspiration and has influenced me even to this day. As I grew in Christ during my time working with Terrie, she invited me and my husband, Jerry, to lead a class at her church's Bible center, which she had founded. (When did she sleep?)

Terrie was a dynamo and definitely about her Father's business. When I think of her smile, I think of Philippians 1:3: "I thank my God upon every remembrance of you" (KJV).

POWER MOVE

Is there a godly sister on your job you can confide in? Pray with? If not, ask God to send you a caring, big-hearted Christian woman who has your best interests at heart and wants to see you prosper at work. We all need a sounding board and someone to keep us accountable on the job. Look for a kindred spirit today.

MY CONFESSION

I thank God for my sisters in Christ at work and want to continue to be a godly example for other women.

27

Daughter, Where Art Thou?

God Never Turns His Back on Us

Then the man and his wife heard the sound of the Lord God as he was walking in the garden in the cool of the day, and they hid from the Lord God among the trees of the garden. But the Lord God called to the man, "Where are you?"

Genesis 3:8–9

Sin is a fact of life. Romans 3:23 says, "All have sinned and fall short of the glory of God." Since the fall of man in the Garden of Eden, when sin entered the human race, mankind has continued to struggle with it. But I thank God for Jesus, whose shed blood allows us to become reunited with God. "For the wages of sin is death, but the gift of God is eternal life in Christ Jesus our Lord" (Rom. 6:23).

When we enjoy a close walk with God and get tripped up in sin, we may feel ashamed, remorseful, or even depressed. But even though we may *feel* like we are separated from God because of our transgression, the truth of the matter is, we can never be separated from him, according to Romans 8:38–39: "For I am convinced that neither death nor life, neither angels nor demons, neither the present nor the future, nor any powers, neither height nor depth, nor anything else in all creation, will be able to separate us from the love of God that is in Christ Jesus our Lord." That pretty much covers everything!

I know of a woman whose affair cost her a terrific job. An attractive woman in her thirties, Barbara (not her real name) was married to a wonderful, godly man and had two beautiful children. A smart, handsome, and charismatic co-worker had been innocently flirting with her for weeks. She resisted his charms, but one day after a Christmas party, they gave in to their mutual desires. One night of passion turned into several weeks of secret trysts.

The more wrapped up Barbara became with this man, the sloppier they got. One evening after everyone had left the office, they had sexual relations on the company's premises. Little did they know that there was a security camera in the exact room they were in, and the whole steamy affair was caught on tape. Barbara was summoned to her human resources department, where she was questioned for two hours regarding the incident. Her lover had already been interrogated and let go. She was suspended with pay for a month and then fired for inappropriate behavior in the workplace.

Through tears of embarrassment and shame, she explained to her husband what had happened and begged his forgiveness. But despite his anger and hurt, he forgave her, and the slow process of rebuilding trust in her marriage began. It was a painful lesson for Barbara to learn, but she confided in me that the worst part of everything was the *perceived* isolation she felt from God. She felt the Lord had abandoned her because of her adultery.

Is the Holy Spirit grieved when we sin? For sure. Are there consequences for our sin? We know there are. But does God provide forgiveness and restoration to us when we sin? Absolutely! It's a trick of Satan to think that God doesn't love us anymore and has banished us from the kingdom. The enemy *wants* us to doubt God and the power of his love and forgiveness. Remember how he tricked Eve (Gen. 3:1). Don't buy into his lies.

POWER MOVE

All of us sin every day. There are sins of omission (the things we know we should do but don't) and sins of commission (the ones we actually commit). But every day, God is with you. He said he'd never leave you or forsake you (Heb. 13:5). So take him at his word.

MY CONFESSION

Even when I sin, I know the Lord will forgive me if I repent and turn away from it. He will never leave me.

28

Family First

Your #1 Ministry

A wife of noble character who can find? She is worth far more than rubies. Her husband has full confidence in her and lacks nothing of value.

PROVERBS 31:10–11

When I went back to work at a local newspaper, my sons David and Jerry were only five months old and three years old, respectively. My mother-in-law quit her job to care for my boys—what a godsend she was. But when I came home, I still had to cook dinner, give the kids their baths, and put them down for bed. At the end of the evening, I was pooped. I used to refer to my home life as "my second job," because that's what it felt like.

As the boys got older, they became independent in some ways, and things got a little easier for me. However, the homework, school projects, and weekend activities (including church) put me back in first gear again. No matter how tired we were, my husband and I were always diligent about attending parent-teacher conferences and staying on top of the boys' grades. All the teachers and principals knew us.

But these sacrifices we made for our family—all the hard work, the sleepless nights, the shouting matches, the money and time spent—led to decent kids who love God and family and turned out okay. My son Jerry won the Thorpe Award for excellence as a high school linebacker, and my husband and I got teary during his speech when he mentioned that his dad had never missed a single football game since his seventh grade year. And David is one of the most compassionate, committed, and loyal people I've ever known. I'm proud to call both of them my sons.

The Lord knows that jobs will come and go, but our children are a gift from him (Ps. 127:3). Your work will absorb as much time as you will give it. But families cannot wait forever, and children grow up with or without you. Invest your time wisely.

POWER MOVE

Being a working mom is hard, so enlist help. You can't do it all and shouldn't have to. If you're single, a relative, neighbor, or friend may be able to lend a hand. Make the time to be there for your kids no matter how inconvenient it may seem. They grow up quickly and remember everything—the school concerts you attended, the stories you read to them when they were three years old, and the special birthday celebrations (including dinners).

MY CONFESSION

My family is my first ministry, and my commitment is to them and to building our family's legacy.

29

God Has a Plan for Your Life

Don't Second-Guess Yourself

> "For I know the plans I have for you," declares the Lord, "plans to prosper you and not to harm you, plans to give you hope and a future."
>
> Jeremiah 29:11

As a young wife and mother, I often had bouts of wondering if I'd made the right choice in marrying at age twenty-five. Our son Jerry Jr. was two years old when my husband and I tied the knot, so we were going into the marriage with a ready-made family—and ready-made responsibility. A year after we got married, I had David. So by age twenty-six, I had two kids and a husband. I loved my family dearly and knew they were a blessing, but at times self-doubt crept in. I wondered, *What if I had waited to get married? What if I'd waited to have another child?* A million scenarios crossed my mind.

What brought on all these thought patterns? I was coveting the fabulous lives of my friends. I didn't realize how ungodly these thoughts were at the time! From my perspective, all of my unmarried, childless friends were living the life—traveling to exotic locales, making good money (for entry-level jobs), being active members of their civic and fraternal organizations, and partying up a storm. It made me wonder where I'd "gone wrong."

I wasn't blaming anyone for my life. I chose to be a single mother. I chose to get married. I chose to have another baby. No one forced my life on me. I chose it, which made me feel even more at fault.

But now, twenty-five years later, I have two wonderful, adult sons I wouldn't give up for the world. I enjoyed every moment of parenting them and don't feel like I really sacrificed much. Some of my girlfriends are married with school-age children, while my husband and I are free to travel and go out whenever we like, even on weeknights, without having to worry about babysitters.

As I reflect on my life now, I realize that God's plan for it is just right. As usual, he works things out perfectly.

POWER MOVE

God's timing is perfect, and everything he does is for a reason. "There is a time for everything, and a season for every activity under heaven" (Eccles. 3:1). So don't burden your spirit with what-ifs. Rest in the assurance that you are exactly where you should be because God has your life in his hands.

MY CONFESSION

Despite my circumstances or how things may appear, I thank God that I am exactly where I should be.

30

Through the Fire

How to Come through Hardship as Pure Gold

Not only so, but we also rejoice in our sufferings, because we know that suffering produces perseverance; perseverance, character; and character, hope.

Romans 5:3–4

One thing is certain: at least once in our lives, we will experience hardship. Even Jesus confirms that our lives on earth won't be free of heartache and pain. "In this world you will have trouble. But take heart! I have overcome the world" (John 16:33).

At one time or another, we've all doubted that God was really with us. It's easy to trust and believe in him when things are going great—all is well on the job, you've got money in the bank, your marriage or relationship is thriving, your children are doing well in school, and you're healthy and growing spiritually. But what happens when you get upsetting news from the doctor? Or your teenage daughter tells you she's pregnant? Or your spouse leaves you for another woman? When your heart is broken, when you've been let down by a family member or friend, when you've experienced loss, it's harder to trust in the Lord.

In Mark 9, when Jesus came upon a demon-possessed boy and his father, he told the man that anything is possible to him who believes (v. 23). The father said, "I do believe; help me overcome my unbelief!" (v. 24). I'm sure there's been a similar time in your job when you doubted God was anywhere in sight. The new boss is on your case every minute for no reason at all. Your co-worker, once considered a friend, betrays your trust. You're in the midst of a mess, and you wonder, *Lord, are you there?* The heart believes, but the flesh, which is weak, doubts.

The Word tells us to trust in the Lord with all our hearts and not place any strength in our own understanding (Prov. 3:5). Trials and hardships are the times when we need God the most and must trust him every step of the way. I can testify that we will be stronger, smarter, tougher, and more lovable at the end. And our fiery experiences will always bless us in some way—to build our faith, our character, our self-esteem, and our anointing.

The funny thing is, God knows the outcome of a situation before it even arises. But he wants *us* to see his power and deliverance in action. He knows what he can do; he wants us to know it also.

POWER MOVE

No matter how tough the trial, you can come out of the fire as Shadrach, Meshach, and Abednego did (Dan. 3:26). Nebuchadnezzar saw "four men, untied and walking around in the midst of the fire! No harm has come to them! And the appearance of the fourth is like that of a god!" (v. 25 NET). Jesus was that fourth man! Remember to call on him, especially during tough times. Sister, your suffering is but for a season. Look to your future and spend your time planning for it.

MY CONFESSION

As I walk through the firestorms of life with the Lord at my side, the flames of doubt and fear will not touch me. I will emerge as pure gold!

31

Signs and Wonders

Believe in Miracles for Yourself and Your Co-workers

God did extraordinary miracles through Paul,
so that even handkerchiefs and aprons that had
touched him were taken to the sick, and their
illnesses were cured and the evil spirits left them.

ACTS 19:11–12

I believe there are no coincidences when it comes to God. We may not know exactly what he's doing at the time (and we may never know), but he knows at all times. Sometimes God will use us to further the gospel in very natural ways. But sometimes he uses us in supernatural ways—even at work.

I remember one co-worker, a middle-aged Jewish woman, who claimed to be an atheist. Beth (not her real name) didn't go to temple or observe the Jewish holidays and customs my other Jewish friends diligently kept.

Beth had a daughter who was in college in Boston at the time. One Tuesday she told me that her daughter, who was only about nineteen, had a cyst on her neck that kept growing, and the doctors thought it might be a malignant tumor.

They planned to remove it the next day to test it, so Beth planned to take the train to Boston to be with her daughter during the surgery.

There was worry and pain in Beth's voice as she told me the story. I tried to console her by telling her that her daughter would be fine; she just had to believe. Beth knew I was a born-again Christian and my positive outlook was part of the faith I represented, so she only smiled and said, "Okay, Carol, if you say so."

My church always had Tuesday night Bible study and began with prayer. That night, I told the church members about my friend's daughter. We asked for complete healing for her and that no tumor would be found. We all agreed in prayer and then continued with our Bible study.

The next day at the office, Beth walked in with a shocked look on her face.

"What are you doing here? I thought you'd be in Boston," I said.

She paused for a second, then said, "The doctor called me late last night and said not to come. He could not find any lump on my daughter's neck. It's gone! So there will be no operation."

Well, I couldn't contain myself. I shouted, "Hallelujah! Glory to God!" I knew that God had heard our prayers and answered them. My colleagues didn't know, but I did. My boss said, "Oh, Carol, it sounds like church in here," turned up her nose, and left in a huff. But that day, I knew my God had come through! And if she wanted to insult me for rejoicing in that miracle, so be it. I would take one for the team—God's team.

To me, it was no coincidence that God would heal the daughter of this woman—this atheist. And it was no coincidence that Beth shared with me—a believer—her family's dilemma. God knew I'd pray and ask others to pray as well. That prayer was the best way I could minister.

God is interested in using you as well.

POWER MOVE

God will use you if you ask him to. It may be something small, such as getting a person to think more about spiritual things or beginning to read the Bible again. Or it may be something larger, such as leading someone to Christ (the biggest miracle of all!) or seeing a healing. Whether it's big or small, God wants to use you to further his kingdom. Whatever role he wants you to play, know that it is important. Be ready, be willing, and be available.

MY CONFESSION

I believe in miracles for my life and others' lives. I will be receptive to the Holy Spirit and allow God to use me as a vessel.

32

Sleep on It

Don't Make Hasty Decisions When You're Angry

Do you see a man who speaks in haste? There is more hope for a fool than for him.

Proverbs 29:20

Picture this. You're a director, and it's time for the annual review of two of your top managers. You did not hire these people, you inherited them—they've been with the company a long time. You've not been privy to their salary history. When your boss gives you the new salary levels and pay raises to share with them at their review, you make a chilling discovery: both of these managers' salaries are higher than yours. You've led, guided, and managed your staff with integrity and respect, but now you feel cheated. So what do you do?

A. Throw a few choice words at your boss and ask her if she's lost her mind.
B. Threaten to quit.
C. Wait a day or two and then decide your next plan of action.

Even though you may want to do A or B, C is the response I think the Lord would want us to have. You need to "come down" and cool off before you discuss it. Take the time to pray about it and ask God for direction.

At one time or another, we've all let our emotions get the best of us and said or did things we didn't mean to. It may have been through an email, a letter, a voice-mail message, or even a face-to-face confrontation. Anger is usually at the root of such confrontations, and the outcome is often not good. When we are angry, we can say things in haste that we may regret later. James 1:19–20 says, "Everyone should be quick to listen, slow to speak and slow to become angry, for man's anger does not bring about the righteous life that God desires." Remember that it's impossible to take back harsh words and deeds.

POWER MOVE

We are a passionate people, but in the workplace we have to bridle our tongues in certain situations, or our reputations (and witness) could be compromised. It's tough sometimes, but we have the greater one abiding in us (1 John 4:4). That's not to say we won't speak in anger. I've certainly done this and regretted it later. But we're only human, and the best thing we can do is apologize for our ugly outbursts. That's why it's so important to stay "prayed up" every day (1 Thess. 5:17). The enemy is seeking whom he can devour (1 Peter 5:8), and you may be his target if you're spiritually vulnerable.

MY CONFESSION

I will not allow my anger to destroy my witness or my good reputation. I will not give the devil a foothold.

33

Lord, What Am I Doing Here?

You're Exactly Where You're Supposed to Be

I wait for the LORD, my soul waits,
and in his word I put my hope.

PSALM 130:5

We've all been there at one time or another on our jobs. You're experiencing a place of dryness with no sign of growth anywhere. You're restless and bored and probably wondering, "What am I doing here?" You may have even tried desperately to look for another job, but to no avail. Despite your various attempts to break free, you're stuck. You may not get the answer right away, but rest assured that God knows exactly why you are in a certain position, in a certain job, at a certain time, for "there is a time for everything, and a season for every activity under heaven" (Eccles. 3:1).

I remember my own experience while employed as a senior copywriter for an African American book club. I had been a copywriter for most of my adult career and found it satisfying, but I was ready to move on. I'd just gotten a certificate of merit for a direct-mail piece I'd written, so I was flying high . . . yet bored. The work, though enjoyable, was no longer challenging. Strict marketing objectives stifled my creativity, but I just went with the flow and basically did what management wanted. I sought other employment but came up with zilch. No bites whatsoever. Little did I know that my blessing—and dream job—was right around the corner.

The editor-in-chief of the book club resigned, and she recommended that I take her place. And now this is a place where I continue to grow and be creative. So there was a reason for me to be in that place at that time.

Your blessing may be right around the corner too. God wants to give it to you. Will you wait for it?

POWER MOVE

You don't know what God has in store for you, but believe it has to be something good. There are no circumstances—only opportunities for learning, growth, and blessing. It's up to us to wait on God and see what good things he has up his sleeve!

MY CONFESSION

I walk by faith and not by sight. What looks like a mistake to me may be exactly the blessing God has in store for me. I will wait on the Lord.

34

Use It or Lose It

Why Your Daily Devotions Are Important

Study to shew thyself approved unto God, a
workman that needeth not to be ashamed,
rightly dividing the word of truth.

2 Timothy 2:15 KJV

When I start my day with prayer and devotion to God, I feel energized and ready to take on the world. Days without some kind of communion with the Lord just don't go right. I get cranky and easily offended, sometimes even cynical.

I remember when I first became a Christian, I was on fire for God. Every morning my feet hit the floor, I said, "Thank you, Jesus!" My prayers were peppered with Scripture: "Lord, you said in your Word that no weapon formed against me shall prosper (Isa. 54:17). . . . I ask you to heal our dear sister ___________, and I claim that by Jesus's stripes she is healed (Isa. 53:5)." And on and on I'd go. I think the reason my prayer life back then was so fruitful was because I studied the Word on a daily basis. As I matured in Christ, I had a good handle on Scripture and took pride in my knowledge of it.

Then my career and family life got busier and more demanding, and I got lazy and stopped studying like I used to because I thought I "knew it." Before long, my accuracy was off. I forgot words, phrases, or entire verses. Sure, the Word was in my heart, but my command of it was not as strong. As a student of the Bible, I was ashamed of my shortcomings because I knew better, so I knew I had to redeem myself—or remain a C student and be poorer for it. So I developed new habits of studying early in the morning, when it was quiet and everyone else in the house was asleep.

It's easy to get sidetracked once your day starts. You can count on the enemy throwing obstacles in your way—phone calls, meetings, friends dropping by. You must study and meditate on the Word daily (Josh. 1:8) or you'll be handicapped spiritually. Some say it takes seven days to develop a habit, so make devotion time a habit if you haven't already. It doesn't have to be long. It can be fifteen minutes of prayer, reading your Bible, and journaling. God wants to hear from you!

POWER MOVE

Make time every day to read and study God's Word. Your devotion time will prepare you for your day at work. You will gain a better knowledge of Scripture and be able to share the Word with others. As you sup with God in your quiet time, allow the Holy Spirit to speak to you through the Word, and then prepare yourself to hear. If it's an hour, a half hour, or even fifteen minutes, time with God is time well spent.

MY CONFESSION

I will make time for my devotions with the Lord, no matter how busy I am.

35

Avon Calling?

When to Keep Your Outside Interests Away from the Workplace

Everything should be done in a fitting and orderly way.

1 Corinthians 14:40

So many of us, especially women, use our workplace to pitch our outside interests—be it selling cosmetics, hawking Girl Scout cookies for our daughters, or soliciting pledges for our walkathons. We're more than eager to sell to our co-workers. Why? Because we have a built-in clientele. First, we know they get paid regularly, so they can afford to buy what we're selling. Second, they have to face us every day, so they won't skip out if they owe us money!

Remember, you are in someone else's place of business. Soliciting on the premises is risky, and you could face disciplinary action—or be fired. An employer may see your Avon or Mary Kay business as competition that takes you away from your duties during working hours. They may see your priorities as being misplaced. The Bible admonishes us to "give to Caesar what is Caesar's" (Mark 12:17), so during work hours, your time belongs to "Caesar" (your boss). After that, your time is your own.

A colleague of mine recently sent out an email asking for a cash donation for her son's struggling athletic program. Her email was sent during business hours with the subject "Need Help." While the purpose was legitimate and her intentions were good, the email was highly inappropriate. Worse yet, she sent out a follow-up email when she didn't receive enough responses!

If you are going to pitch your business to friends at work, do so discreetly. Post your Girl Scout cookie sign-up sheet in a common area, like a break room. Leave brochures for Avon or Mary Kay in the ladies' room. That way you're not pushing your business on colleagues and making them feel uncomfortable or pressured to support you.

POWER MOVE

Having a side business is fine, but be careful not to violate your company's "no solicitation" rule. You can easily invite a few friends over to your home or contact them during non-business hours. The Lord wants us to prosper in every way, but he doesn't want us to disregard or disrespect policies at work.

MY CONFESSION

I will respect my company's policies regarding soliciting on my job. I desire the Lord's blessing on all my ventures, so I will do what's right.

36

"Put Some Weight on the Bar"

Exercise Your Faith and Strengthen Your Spirit

I tell you the truth, if you have faith as small as
a mustard seed, you can say to this mountain,
"Move from here to there" and it will move.
Nothing will be impossible for you.

MATTHEW 17:20

Our faith is like a muscle. The more we exercise it, the more it grows and becomes stronger. The less we exercise it, the more spiritually weak we become. If you can believe God for the small, everyday things most people take for granted (air, water, shelter, and food), you can believe him for miracles. Do you believe God for huge blessings—your own business, a big raise or promotion, added staff?

Years ago I entered a power-lifting competition. Joe, a friend and co-worker, was a power lifter himself and had won many trophies in the dead-lift category by pulling hundreds of pounds off the floor. He and I worked out regularly with another friend of ours. He remarked how easily weight lifting came to me and suggested I enter the next power-lifting meet in our area. I'd never entered anything competitively before, and I was a bit nervous about the prospect of competing with other women who were stronger and more experienced weight lifters than I was. But I thought, *I have nothing to lose, and it will be fun.*

After a few weeks of training with Joe, the meet was upon us. When it was my first turn to lift, Joe loaded the barbell with 180 pounds—my opener. I easily pulled the bar to my knees until the referee yelled, "Down!" which meant I could release the bar. For my second pull, Joe loaded 200 pounds, and I hoisted the bar up to my knees.

At that point, a friend who regularly lifted with us at the gym pulled Joe aside. "Joe," I heard him half whisper, "that was nothing for her. Put some weight on the bar. She can do it." I glanced over at Joe, and he was deep in thought. I could tell he was considering how many more plates he could add to the 200 pounds that I'd just pulled.

Next thing I knew, the plates were loaded and I was back up on the lifting platform. Once the ref signaled me to begin my lift, I could tell it would be a challenge. I grunted and pulled until the bar was at my knees, well off the ground, as the crowd roared and cheered me on to complete my lift. "Down!" was the sweetest word I'd ever heard.

After the lift, Joe smiled and told me he'd added another 50 pounds to the 200, not the extra 25 we had agreed on. I had doubled my own expectations! And not only was 250 pounds my best lift ever, but I won second place!

The Lord showed me that I can do more than I'd ever thought possible. If Joe had asked me, "Do you think you can pull 250?" I probably would have just said, "No, go with the 225. I know I can pull that." Thank God he didn't ask me. He just loaded the bar and told me to pull.

God does the same thing with us. If he wanted to get our permission for every little thing, we wouldn't get much accomplished because our faith would have no room to grow.

It would be stagnant. That 250-pound victory increased my faith by showing me that I can exceed my own expectations if I only believe. I lifted for God, and he lifted me up. If you want to see God move mightily on your behalf, put some weight on the bar!

POWER MOVE

In what area of your life do you need to push your faith a bit more, or "put some weight on the bar"? Take stock of the things in life you really want—and shore up your faith to believe you can receive those things. We have a loving Father who wants his children to believe they can have anything they ask for in prayer (Matt. 21:22).

MY CONFESSION

My faith is getting stronger by the day. I will exceed my reach and believe God will bless and prosper me.

37

"Don't Even Go There!"

Keep Your Mind Free from Negativity

> The peace of God, which transcends all understanding, will guard your hearts and your minds in Christ Jesus.
>
> Philippians 4:7

One of my favorite sayings is, "It's okay for the birds to fly over your head, but it's not okay for them to nest there." The truth is, you cannot stop negative thoughts from coming at you, but you have the ability to "swat" them away and not let them take up residence in your spirit. If you allow one destructive thought to enter your spirit and live there, it will make itself at home—so make every effort to abolish thoughts of unworthiness, doubt, fear, and worry before they nest in your mind. God will give you peace when you do. "Thou wilt keep him in perfect peace, whose mind is stayed on thee, because he trusteth in thee" (Isa. 26:3 KJV).

You don't have to be a new believer to be tempted with evil thoughts. Even the strongest, most faithful Christian will find thoughts of fear and doubt creeping in. No matter how positive you remain, how hopeful your outlook on life, situations may occur that make you question yourself, other people, and even God. But the real test is whether you accept negative circumstances as just that—a temporary blip on the screen—or gloom and doom forever.

The Bible says not to give the devil a foothold (Eph. 4:27). Those footholds begin in your head. Even the greatest men of the Bible such as David wrestled with negative thoughts: "How long must I wrestle with my thoughts and every day have sorrow in my heart? How long will my enemy triumph over me?" (Ps. 13:2). But David never let negative thoughts be the last word. He always turned to praise: "I will bless the LORD at all times; his praise shall continually be in my mouth" (Ps. 34:1 KJV). We must do the same. When the fiery darts are thrown at your head, hold up your shield of faith and tell the devil, "Don't even go there!"

POWER MOVE

When thoughts such as "I can't," "I won't," or "I'll never" enter your mind, realize they are simply Satan's way of deterring you from the work God would have you to do, on the job or outside of it. Think only of the good God has blessed you with. "Finally, brothers, whatever is true, whatever is noble, whatever is right, whatever is pure, whatever is lovely, whatever is admirable—if anything is excellent or praiseworthy—think about such things" (Phil. 4:8). Write out this and other positive, life-affirming Scriptures and post them where you can see them at work. The best defense is a good offense!

MY CONFESSION

I will keep my spirit and my mind free from negativity—I will not even go there!

38

Get Over It

Let Go of Past Mistakes and Missteps

Forget the former things; do not dwell on the past. See, I am doing a new thing! Now it springs up; do you not perceive it? I am making a way in the desert and streams in the wasteland.

Isaiah 43:18–19

"Everybody makes mistakes. That's why there are erasers on pencils!" My mother always said this statement with such conviction that she more than convinced me it was true. So why do we agonize over our past mistakes and missteps? Guilt. Embarrassment. Shame. Remorse. Whatever the reason, God wants us to admit our mistakes, learn from them, and then *forget* them. Chances are, you'll make so many mistakes during the course of your lifetime that you'll never be able to count them all anyway. "There is not a righteous man on earth who does what is right and never sins" (Eccles. 7:20). So why keep a running tally?

When I was working at the newspaper, my department created a flyer for the circulation department. It was a rush job, and I worked feverishly to meet our end-of-day deadline—writing the copy, getting it approved by the circulation director, verifying the statistics with our research team, and getting the art finalized with the art director. I was the project manager and was responsible for all aspects of the job, from concept to completion. But in my quest to get the job done and to the printer, I had forgotten to check one little detail: the phone number. It wasn't our standard phone number (I knew that one by heart); it was the number to one of our satellite offices in New York City. It turns out I had transposed two of the digits. I thought the circ managers had checked the number, and they thought I had. Ultimately, it was my responsibility.

Several thousand copies of that flyer went to potential subscribers all over the city. Every person who called the number to start home delivery realized they hadn't reached the newspaper at all—they'd reached a Chinese takeout in Queens! It's funny now, but I wasn't laughing at the time. And neither was my boss. Whenever a complaint letter arrived, she simply dropped it on my desk. The sting of that error lasted for weeks. I was embarrassed and ashamed and saw the mistake as a reflection of my ability as a manager. My boss saw it as a reflection (a bad one) of her department.

After the first few letters, I got a tougher skin about the mistake. Yes, it was a mistake. Yes, I made it. And yes, it was over and done with! There were many more projects to be executed, so I couldn't dwell on that one mistake any longer. If my boss wanted to act childishly, that was her prerogative. But I had work to do and wasn't about to let one incident define me as a manager.

Thank God he does not hold our sins and mistakes against us. "If you, O LORD, kept a record of sins, O Lord, who could stand?" (Ps. 130:3).

POWER MOVE

We're all guilty of mistakes. Some are more grievous than others, and the repercussions and consequences differ. But don't let past mistakes hold your spirit hostage, whether it's on the job or off. If you make a mistake, fix it if you can, apologize if it's necessary, and move on. People may not forgive you, but God will.

MY CONFESSION

I will not let the mistakes and missteps of the past hold me hostage. I press onward and upward!

39

Gossip Girls

Staying Away from Toxic Co-workers

Do not spread false reports. Do not help a wicked man by being a malicious witness.

Exodus 23:1

Even the most "innocent" piece of gossip hurts someone's reputation, credibility, or character. So why do we gossip? Because we're not the victim; someone else is.

We're all guilty of gossiping. But in the workplace, we should steer clear of others who are talking too much about other people's lives. Here's why:

- **They can't be trusted.** "A gossip betrays a confidence, but a trustworthy man keeps a secret" (Prov. 11:13). Nothing is worse than having your business put out in the street by someone you thought was a friend, someone who is so eager to get a reaction and stir up some negative dialogue that your secrets are the last thing she wants to keep under wraps. Be selective about sharing personal issues about yourself that you don't want made public by a gossip girl.
- **They come between friends.** "A perverse man stirs up dissension, and a gossip separates close friends" (Prov. 16:28). My mother always said, "A dog that brings a

bone will carry a bone," which is Southern wisdom meaning a person who gossips about others will gossip about you too. You just need to give them enough ammunition. Longtime friendships have busted up, romances have fizzled, and family members have become estranged because of "he said, she said" situations.

- **Their words cut deeply.** "The words of a gossip are like choice morsels; they go down to a man's inmost parts" (Prov. 18:8). Words have the power to either bless or curse—and both go deep into your spirit. Psalm 64:2–3 says, "Hide me from the conspiracy of the wicked, from that noisy crowd of evildoers. They sharpen their tongues like swords and aim their words like deadly arrows." They know their words will hurt you, and that's why they say them. True friends they are not!
- **They are troublemakers.** "Without wood a fire goes out, without gossip a quarrel dies down" (Prov. 26:20). I'm sure you have a friend or relative who's always in the middle of a mess. This happens a lot in large families, but the same principle applies at work. Miss Busybody scoots from office to office and cubicle to cubicle, gathering information like a squirrel gathers nuts, and then she starts blabbering about what she's seen and heard. Once again she's at the root of a disagreement because of her big mouth.
- **They have hidden motives.** "Like a coating of glaze over earthenware are fervent lips with an evil heart" (Prov. 26:23). There's one in every workplace: the woman who latches onto you like a fly on sticky paper, acts like she's your very best friend, and tells you how much she loves you two days after meeting you. She's a fixture at your desk every day and calls or emails you several times a day. Worse yet, she demands to know your every

move, asking you a bunch of personal questions, but she doesn't volunteer any information about herself. You notice that she's close with some of the most gossipy, disgruntled employees at work. They're unhappy people, and she fits right in with them. No matter how friendly she seems, her actions are not those of a friend.

- **They waste your time.** "They get into the habit of being idle and going about from house to house. And not only do they become idlers, but also gossips and busybodies, saying things they ought not to" (1 Tim. 5:13). Beware of co-workers who seem to have a lot of time on their hands. You may see them wandering the halls, chitchatting in someone's cubicle, or lounging in the break room. "They are not busy; they are busybodies" (2 Thess. 3:11). And while you might have great lunch conversations, your association with them will not help you in the long run.

POWER MOVE

Now's the time to cut off the gossipers. And stop engaging in gossip yourself. Your gossiping buddies will see you aren't going to play that game with them anymore, and they'll stop coming by your office or desk to chat. You may lose this bunch of "frenemies" as lunch buddies, but at least your conscience will be clear—and your spirit will be free of that negativity.

MY CONFESSION

Lord, help me to bridle my tongue when it comes to unhealthy, ungodly talk and associations with those who tear others down with their words. Let the words of my mouth be acceptable in your sight.

40

Take a Load Off

Find Time for Yourself Every Day

By the seventh day God had finished the work he had been doing; so on the seventh day he rested from all his work.

Genesis 2:2

Just about every woman's magazine stresses the importance of taking care of ourselves. All women, especially black women, take on way too much. We try to be the Proverbs 31 woman of the Bible—work full-time, raise a family, be active in church, sit on community boards, be active in our sororities—all while keeping a smile on our faces. But the truth is, we're burned-out, depressed, sleep-deprived, overworked, and stressed out from juggling all of those priorities.

Genesis 2:2 puts everything in perspective. The almighty God, in his infinite wisdom, decided to rest after creating the heavens and the earth. His was a task that would last for eternity, and it was more important than anything else. But think about it: God didn't *need* to rest; he *chose* to. "God blessed the seventh day and made it holy, because on it he rested from all the work of creating that he had done" (Gen. 2:3). I think the Lord was trying to show us that we all need to recharge our batteries, no matter how busy we are. Even Jesus took breaks and retreated to a quiet place.

I've always had a love for film, and in the early nineties

I joined the Black Filmmaker Foundation, an organization for filmmakers, screenwriters, and those aspiring to become such. Our monthly meetings were held in New York City's Greenwich Village on Saturdays. I looked forward to it every month, because not only did I get to make important connections, but I also made new friends. We'd go out after the meetings to a little burger joint called Eddie's and talk about the projects we were working on.

No matter how late I got home, I noticed I was full of energy. I loved it because it was my only time to focus on my interests, goals, and dreams and have a semblance of a social life outside of church and work. It was my only "me" time when I didn't have to worry about cooking, cleaning, or attending to my preschool boys.

Every woman needs some time of her own. So take yours!

POWER MOVE

Admit that you cannot do it all, and ask for help. You are not a failure—you're human, and human bodies get tired, get sick, and will eventually give out. It's an old cliché, but how can you care for others if you're out of commission? The entire household will suffer. So get your sleep (at least seven hours), take your vitamins, and exercise for at least fifteen minutes per day (this releases endorphins, the "feel-good" hormone). Also, do at least one thing for yourself every day: read a book or magazine for an hour, take a luxurious bath after the kids are asleep, listen to your favorite tunes on your iPod, or just do . . . nothing.

MY CONFESSION

I will recharge my batteries every day no matter how much I have to do.

41

Returning to Work

Making the Transition from Home to Office

She gets up while it is still dark; she
provides food for her family.

PROVERBS 31:15

I remember the first day I went back to work after my youngest son David was born. He was only five months old but had already been hospitalized twice. My oldest son Jerry was only three years old and not quite ready for preschool. But I had a bachelor's degree in communications and wanted to use it. Besides, we needed the money.

I had prayed long and hard and felt that if it was God's will, I would return to work. He knew me—he'd made me, after all—and he knew that I'd been working since I was fourteen years old. My mother-in-law had quit her job to watch the kids, and that was a major blessing. (I may have turned down the job if she hadn't agreed to do that.) Although I was offered a great job with good benefits and decent pay, I still had feelings of anxiety. I felt the Lord had blessed me with this job, but was I doing the right thing?

As I sat in my new office, I imagined my routine—the usual times I'd give Jerry Jr. his snack and David his bath, or when I'd start dinner. I got misty over those great memories, but I knew I was doing this to better our family's situation in the long run. We'd have two salaries now, and we'd be able to move out of our rental house with its leaky roof and drafty windows and start saving for a home of our own.

Yet I wondered how my returning to work would affect Jerry Jr. and David. Was I depriving them of love and attention because I wasn't home anymore? Would they want to be with their grandmother more than me? I knew I was probably being paranoid, but I couldn't help it. Both my mother and my mother-in-law had stayed home with their children while their husbands provided for the household, so Jerry Sr. and I had both had the privilege of being raised by stay-at-home moms. But that was the sixties, when the only jobs for uneducated black women were as domestics and nannies. I had a college degree and a lot more career opportunities. I wanted my children to be in a better position socially, financially, and spiritually than I had been. But that would take sacrifice on someone's part—mine.

As it turned out, I was more diligent about mothering them after I returned to work than I was when I was a stay-at-home mom. We all sat down and ate dinner together every night, and I read to them and prayed with them every night. I was glad to see them, and they were happy to see me. Absence really does make the heart grow fonder, even with children!

That was over twenty years ago, and I don't regret any of it because I know I did my best. Were there challenges to working outside the home? Absolutely—almost on a regular basis. But with God's grace, a supportive family, and sheer determination to provide a more comfortable lifestyle for my children, my transition from stay-at-home mom to back-to-work mom was a fruitful and productive one.

POWER MOVE

Ask God what his will is for you and your family. Sometimes your motives are pure but aren't in sync with God's timing. Maybe he's preparing you for a greater ministry right at home, so the career door will be closed. Be sensitive to the Holy Spirit and his leading. "For as many as are led by the Spirit of God, they are the sons of God" (Rom. 8:14 KJV).

MY CONFESSION

My family comes first, so I will seek God's guidance in every decision concerning them.

42

Girl, Watch Your Mouth!

Positive Confession Equals Positive Results

Death and life are in the power of the tongue:
and they that love it shall eat the fruit thereof.

PROVERBS 18:21 KJV

"I'll never get anywhere." "My job stinks." "These people hate me." "There are no good black men out there." If you haven't made these negative comments yourself, I'm sure you've heard someone else speak them.

We've all said things we didn't mean—in anger, jealousy, or fear—and regretted every misspoken word. We wish we could take back the words, but they are unleashed into the spiritual realm as well as the physical one. That's not to say that if you speak one negative word, your life is doomed. It is not. I believe it's the constant barrage of negativity that comes out of our mouths that does the most damage. The Word of God says, "Bless and do not curse" (Rom. 12:14). If we speak unfruitful words over our lives or situations, how can we expect God to bless what we've cursed? So think about your language before you even open your mouth.

I had a boss and dear friend who would always preface instructions by saying, "Here's what you'll need to know in case I get hit by a bus." Now, this woman was sweet, positive, and caring—a great boss and human being. Why she'd say something so off the wall I'll never know. I'd hate to think there's a bus roaming around on the earth, looking to hit her!

We must realize that positive words can create positive results in our lives. When I sold Mary Kay cosmetics, my team director would pass out affirmation cards to each sales associate. I was bound to have an off month at times, meaning I didn't meet my goals. That was normal. Those affirmation cards would contain powerful and uplifting "I can" and "I will" statements. The last thing I wanted to do when I was having a slow month in sales was get down on myself.

Positive self-talk helps bolster our confidence. And it begins with our words. "Be not deceived; God is not mocked: for whatsoever a man soweth, that shall he also reap" (Gal. 6:7 KJV). Those who put a negative spin on things naturally attract the worst in life. Misfortune seems to follow them like a magnet.

James 3:8–9 says, "No man can tame the tongue. It is a restless evil, full of deadly poison. With the tongue we praise our Lord and Father, and with it we curse men, who have been made in God's likeness." What do you find yourself saying about your job? Your boss? Words are powerful, and they also have creative power for good. Next time you want to say something negative, think first, then speak. In short, watch your mouth!

POWER MOVE

Your words influence your life, so make sure you're speaking blessings, not curses, over your situation at work. It's tempting to "let loose" on a co-worker or situation on the job, but resist the urge. Take the problem to the Lord in prayer first. He knows the outcome before you even open your mouth.

Then talk it over with a trusted friend who will pray with you about it (Matt. 18:20). You are God's child, and he expects you to rise above the mind-set of the children of the world. "May the words of my mouth and the meditation of my heart be pleasing in your sight, O Lord, my Rock and my Redeemer" (Ps. 19:14).

MY CONFESSION

I am a believer, not a doubter, and will speak only life over my situation at work.

43

Love in the Afternoon

Use Discretion When Dating a Co-worker

Wisdom is more precious than rubies, and
nothing you desire can compare with her.

PROVERBS 8:11

Two couples dated while employed by the same company. Meet Couple #1. From the moment he laid eyes on her, he knew she would be his wife. And her heart fluttered the first time she took his hand after they were introduced by a mutual co-worker. Their eyes locked, and clearly it was love at first sight. But she knew they had to be careful at work—it would be career suicide for her if they weren't discreet. This was a place of business, after all. What would be the point of being in love and unemployed? So this smart sister kept their budding romance under wraps and outside of company walls (and prying eyes) for months, spending time with her honey after work and on weekends. Imagine her co-workers' surprise when she and Mr. Right announced their engagement. "We didn't even know you guys were a couple!" was a comment echoed by many at their wedding reception.

Meet Couple #2. He was an alpha male—handsome, successful, confident, and determined to get what he wanted. So it was no wonder that he was fixated on a pretty new assistant manager—an assertive, caring, but lonely single woman. His quick wit and charm were alluring to her, and her intelligence and gentle nature drew him in. Lunches soon turned into dinners, which turned into weekends spent together. For them, the excitement of an office romance was too exhilarating to pass up—stolen glances in meetings, featherlike touches when "no one" was looking. Before long, they seemed not to care whether other people knew about their romance or not.

Then the rumors started spreading . . . about her. Once she got wind of the hurtful and exaggerated comments her coworkers were saying behind her back, she decided to cut things off with Mr. Successful, who took the news with a grain of salt and soon forgot about her. Her career—and reputation—were damaged because she made a private relationship public at work.

When I've seen this happen, it's usually the man who comes out unscathed and the woman who's left holding the bag. So be cautious. The Bible says, "Like a gold ring in a pig's snout is a beautiful woman who shows no discretion" (Prov. 11:22). Don't be that woman!

POWER MOVE

It's up to you to carefully guard your reputation if you are seeing someone on the job. Don't depend on a man to protect your honor. More than likely he'll be worried about his own bread and butter. Many women have found soul mates in the workplace to whom they've remained happily married, while others have lost jobs, promotions, or reputations because of office affairs gone awry. Love is a beautiful thing, but God wants his daughters to be "wise as serpents, and harmless as doves" (Matt. 10:16 KJV).

MY CONFESSION

I will use wisdom and seek God's guidance in affairs of the heart.

44

Dream On

Make Your Vision a Reality

Commit to the LORD whatever you
do, and your plans will succeed.

PROVERBS 16:3

Surely you have a dream—something God has put in your heart or spirit to create, initiate, or execute during your lifetime. You get so excited just thinking about this "thing" that no matter what you do, you cannot shake it. You know that you and only you can bring this dream to fruition. God gave it to you. It's yours. But understand that a lot of time and space will come between you and your dream. No one who's ever achieved success at anything did so overnight. It took a lot of hard work, time, energy, and determination to get where they wanted to be. They may have made great sacrifices to attain their ultimate goal or live their dream—money, a social life, or even a relationship may have had to take a backseat.

Dr. Martin Luther King Jr. is a prime example of how hard work and sacrifice can bring a dream to pass. Dr. King knew in his heart that segregation was an evil that needed to be eradicated. God gave him the vision, the fortitude, and the energy to spearhead a movement that would change society for future generations. He had a dream of peace, equality, and justice for African Americans and all oppressed people. He never wavered in his message and sustained insults, mistreatment by the police, imprisonment, and eventually death because of his commitment to the dream. You and I continue to enjoy the benefits of his steadfast quest for equality to this day.

Barack Obama is another example. During his historic campaign for president, had he not been committed to his dream of becoming president, he probably would have given up long before. The sleepless nights, the time away from his family, the horrendous traveling schedule, the lies and campaign slurs leveled against him from the opposing side, the death threats—he could have easily said, "It's not worth it," and thrown in the towel. But because he ran the race (1 Cor. 9:24) and did not give up, he became the forty-fourth president of the United States of America and the first African American to hold the post. Mr. Obama's dream came true on November 4, 2008.

What are you dreaming of?

POWER MOVE

Even if you're currently employed in a job just to make ends meet, don't give up on pursuing your dream. Are you a singer? Then book gigs at night or on weekends to showcase your talent and get you the necessary exposure. You'll probably need to make a demo tape, and the extra cash you earn from singing could help pay for it. If you have to skip hanging out with friends on the weekend to work on your book, do it. They may not like it at first, but true friends will understand that you're on a mission. The bottom line is, whatever it is you need to do to turn your dream into reality, do it. You'll also need your family's support every step of the way, so ask for your spouse's help early on while you pursue your dream. And don't be ashamed to ask for help from other family, friends, or co-workers. Your husband may have to cook dinner twice a week, or your mom may have to pick up the kids from day care every Wednesday. If they're willing to help, accept it graciously. The results will pay off in a major way—when you're successful, the whole family will be blessed.

MY CONFESSION

I will pursue my dream with tenacity, commitment, and prayer.

45

Gone Fishin'

How to Really Win Souls

"Come, follow me," Jesus said, "and I will make you fishers of men."

Matthew 4:19

It's not only your pastor's responsibility to lead others to Christ on Sunday morning. There are six other days in the week, and it's up to us as followers of Christ to share the Good News with our fellow man. You don't have to be a pastor, teacher, or evangelist to lead nonbelievers to Christ. And the workplace is an excellent pond to fish in.

In New York City, we have street preachers passing out Bible tracts on the subway or extolling the message of salvation in Times Square. Call them what you may—bold soldiers or Jesus freaks—but I've always admired their holy boldness and secretly wished I could do the same. Yet over the years, as I grew in Christ, I realized God had given me a different approach to evangelism. I'm not an aggressive person by nature. I came to Christ through his message of love and reconciliation, not the fear of hellfire. But I did want to share Jesus with others and let them experience the joy I felt. So I took several evangelism classes to prepare and equip myself, since 2 Timothy 2:15 admonishes us, "Do your best to present yourself to God as one approved, a workman who does not need to be ashamed and who correctly handles the word of truth."

I remember one colleague in particular. Ann (not her real name) was a pretty and smart sales executive who did business with my department. Although she came to call on me for business, we hit it off right away, and our conversations would often drift to juggling motherhood and work. Ann had a lot in common with me: she was a young married mother of two boys also.

After several months, Ann made her usual sales call and asked me why I'd been out of the office so much. I told her that we'd hit rock bottom and lost our home, cars, everything. She expressed how sorry she was, and after seeing how broken I was, she asked me if I was okay. (I wasn't.) I remember telling her how good God was and that if it weren't for him, I'd have surely lost my mind during this whole ordeal. I shared my testimony, which was loaded with Scripture, and everything I learned in those evangelism classes came back to my mind.

I was so broken and emotionally battered, I felt I had nothing to lose in sharing this with Ann. If I got fired, so be it. My life had completely unraveled, so another loss would have been no big deal. So I went for it.

It was a surreal moment—it was like me watching myself witness to Ann. I don't remember much after that, but at that second, I turned sort of fearless, like those street preachers I'd long admired. I simply asked her one question: "Will you accept Jesus Christ as your personal Lord and Savior?" I think we were both surprised when she said, "Yes!" I took her hands, and she recited the prayer of salvation after me. It was a day I'll never forget.

POWER MOVE

Whatever you do—passing out Bible tracts, doing face-to-face witnessing, conducting Bible studies on your employer's premises (after you get permission)—pray and ask God for wisdom. He wants to use us to help build Christ's kingdom, but he also commands that we be mindful of how we conduct ourselves. "Let all things be done decently and in order" (1 Cor. 14:40 KJV).

MY CONFESSION

I will bear witness to Christ through my words, deeds, and actions and lead others to him as the Holy Spirit allows.

46

Don't Be Hatin'

There Are Enough Blessings to Go Around

For where you have envy and selfish ambition,
there you find disorder and every evil practice.

James 3:16

It happens to the best of us. We see another co-worker get a promotion or special recognition, and upon hearing the news, we offer hearty congratulations. At the time, we mean it. But as we start to look at our own lives, we wonder why they got blessed and we didn't. This is especially true if we trained that person or were instrumental in their growth. We feel cheated and ignored. Instead of helping them celebrate, we wonder, *Lord, where is my blessing? Why didn't I get that recognition instead of this person? What about me?* We become impatient, thinking that the Lord has passed over us and dished out the very last promotion, raise, or commendation. We're convinced that the kingdom's "cupboard" is bare. Imagine there being a shortage in God's storehouse—preposterous!

The truth is, there is more than enough of everything to go around. Our God is not a God of lack. He is a God of plenty—plenty of money, plenty of opportunities, plenty of food, plenty of spiritual blessings.

I recall one instance at work when I was having an especially hard day and confided in a co-worker, a woman I considered a friend, about how rough my job was sometimes. I told her that as much as I loved my position, it was stressful and not without its challenges. She listened intently but then rolled her eyes and said, "Well, one monkey don't stop no show." I was more surprised than hurt by her comment. I'd never said I was irreplaceable or that no one else could do my job. I was just venting. So her dig came out of left field.

This co-worker was one of the few sisters at work, and we had bonded pretty quickly. I felt comfortable talking to her about issues at work. I didn't think any less of her after she said what she did; she was still fun to be around and likable. But then I thought about it: I was getting a lot of attention lately—I'd been on a local news show and had the ear of upper management. Although the majority of my co-workers supported and encouraged me, there was a small faction that probably was a bit envious. But I didn't expect it to come from someone I considered a friend.

POWER MOVE

Jesus tells us not to worry about anything because there is plenty to go around. Instead of wasting precious time and mental energy being jealous of a co-worker or friend who just received a blessing, go into your prayer closet and ask the Lord what he would have *you* do. Ask him to show you how to be a better employee. Ask him to put people in your path to mentor and bless you. Rejoice in the fact that you serve a God who doesn't show favoritism (Acts 10:34).

MY CONFESSION

What God has done for others, he can do for me—and more!

47

The Value of Work

God Will Supply All Your Needs

The worker deserves his wages.

1 Timothy 5:18

Because our livelihoods depend on it, money matters. Of course, our education, our work experience, our industry, and other key factors weigh in heavily on how much we will earn. Recent college grads in entry-level positions can't expect to be paid the same amount as someone who's been on the job for ten years. And a neurosurgeon will be better compensated than a general practitioner due to the additional training needed and the complexity of the medical specialty. But what does God say about money? I think that while he would want us to be paid fairly, he wouldn't want us to be fixated on salary alone.

When I got out of college in the early eighties, I took a job as a receptionist at an advertising agency. Advertising, radio, TV, and publishing are considered glamorous fields, and most college grads start at the bottom—as administrative assistants, receptionists, or executive assistants. Basically, I had to "get in where I could fit in" and work my way up through the ranks. That job didn't pay much, but I didn't complain. The apostle Paul said, "I know what it is to be in need, and I know what it is to have plenty. I have learned the secret of being content in any and every situation, whether well fed or hungry, whether living in plenty or in want" (Phil. 4:12). I was living at home with my parents, so my expenses were low. Thank God I wasn't in debt so I was able to give them money for household expenses.

But after I gave birth to my first child, all that changed. I needed a better job with more money. Eventually I got promoted at the agency and made a bit more money, but it was still tough making ends meet. Although I was still living with my parents, I now had to pay for child care, diapers, clothing, and medical costs for my son. I had to budget the amount of money I had. After I got married and moved out of the city, I decided to quit that job. Commuting costs would have eaten a chunk of my pay, so it didn't make sense to continue working in the city with such a small income. Years later, I got a job in the suburb where I lived and finally made decent money with a management position that led to greater pay.

God is depending on us to be good stewards of whatever we have. Our salaries can and will change, but God's expectation of how we use what he gives us will never change.

POWER MOVE

Money is always a consideration when you decide to take a job. It's important that you find out what the going rate is for your position, your level of experience, and even where you live. Do your research and ask God for guidance when it comes to your salary. Jesus says that "your Father knows what you need before you ask him" (Matt. 6:8).

MY CONFESSION

My God shall supply all my needs through his riches in glory.

48

Pray without Ceasing

Keep Your Communication Lines Open with the Lord

Be careful for nothing; but in every thing by prayer and supplication with thanksgiving let your requests be made known unto God.

PHILIPPIANS 4:6 KJV

Jesus spent a huge amount of time in prayer with the Father. He prayed for everything and everyone—for children (Matt. 19:13), for his disciples (John 17:9), for all believers (John 17:20), for deliverance (Matt. 26:39), and even for himself (John 17:1). The Lord knew that open and frequent communication with the Father would be essential to our growth as Christians, and he was our shining example. The Father loves to hear from us, and prayer keeps our spirits open and receptive to the leading and guiding of the Holy Spirit.

Imagine not calling, emailing, or texting your best friend for weeks or even months. You'd miss that person to no end—you would want to know what's new in her life, share her joys and challenges, and help her out if she needed you. You'd be lost without the connection you two once shared. You'd be miserable, and so would she.

I imagine that's how God feels when he doesn't hear from us on a regular basis. He longs to connect with us. He longs to bless us. But communication is never a one-way street. We need to make prayer a priority in our lives, especially at work. Early in my Christian walk, I would spend about a half hour before work praying and asking God for protection for me and my family, my co-workers, my bosses, and the executives who ran the company.

Prayer breaks down strongholds, those tight demonic grips on a situation or person. The famed Brooklyn Tabernacle is known for its twenty-four-hour Prayer Band, a phone-in telephone line with round-the-clock prayer warriors who pray for people in shifts, like a regular job. Because that church has been (and still is) so dedicated to prayer, the congregation has experienced multiple blessings over the years. But God isn't limited to only one church. He wants to hear from all of his children. He says in 2 Chronicles 7:14, "If my people, who are called by my name, will humble themselves and pray and seek my face and turn from their wicked ways, then will I hear from heaven and will forgive their sin and will heal their land."

POWER MOVE

Pray for protection. Ask for the Lord's protection over you and your loved ones. "For he will command his angels concerning you to guard you in all your ways; they will lift you up in their hands, so that you will not strike your foot against a stone" (Ps. 91:11–12). All of Psalm 91 is a good one to recite and commit to memory.

Pray for your family. Your spouse, children, parents, and other relatives need prayer every day. Pray for your spouse, as the head of the household, to make godly decisions concerning the family. Pray over your children—for their safety, their health, and their teachers. "The prayer of a righteous man is powerful and effective" (James 5:16).

Pray for your bosses. Nobody's perfect, and your bosses are no exception. However, you are under their rule, so be respectful (1 Peter 2:13). If they are not Christians, pray they will accept Jesus Christ as their Lord and Savior. If they are Christians, pray the Lord will lead them and guide them in their decisions.

Pray for wisdom. God wants to lead you into all truth, so ask for his wisdom in dealing with situations at work. "Wisdom will save you from the ways of wicked men, from men whose words are perverse" (Prov. 2:12).

Pray for your church and pastor. Lift up your pastor and church on a daily basis. Pray for your pastor's health and for God to give him or her wisdom concerning the congregation and matters of the church. Ask the Lord to bless your ministry and fill it with doers of the Word so that God's kingdom can be built up. "They devoted themselves to the apostles' teaching and to the fellowship, to the breaking of bread and to prayer" (Acts 2:42).

MY CONFESSION

I will keep the lines of communication open between me and the Lord through prayer.

49

What Is Your Vision?

Know Where You're Going So You'll Know How to Get There

Where there is no vision, the people perish.

PROVERBS 29:18 KJV

When Diana Ross sang "Theme from Mahogany (Do You Know Where You're Going To)" back in 1975, I thought it was one of the prettiest ballads I'd ever heard. Even though I was a young girl, the words to that song resonated with me. If you listen to the lyrics closely, you'll see that the song is nostalgic and sad, but in my youthful naïveté, I looked at the song's title in more literal terms—"where do you want to go in life?" God warns us that we cannot predict our future (Eccles. 7:14). However, he confirms that it will be good: "'For I know the plans I have for you,' declares the LORD, 'plans to prosper you and not to harm you, plans to give you hope and a future'" (Jer. 29:11).

We all *think* we know what we are to do in this life and how we intend to get there. The Bible instructs us to make plans but warns us that those plans are tentative and God has the final blueprint for our lives. "In his heart a man plans his course, but the LORD determines his steps" (Prov. 16:9).

POWER MOVE

What is your vision? Do you know what you'd like to do in life? If you're unsure, make a list of your strengths and talents. Sometimes your life's work will evolve out of your skills, not necessarily out of your current job. Now, where do you see yourself in five years? In ten years? In twenty-five years? If you don't know exactly, start jotting down your goals. Then ask God for direction. Whether you're clear on your vision or not, write everything down; no goal is too large for God (Matt. 19:26). You can always refine your list later. Habakkuk 2:2 says, "And the LORD answered me, and said, Write the vision, and make it plain upon tables, that he may run that readeth it" (KJV). Be diligent and work toward your vision every day. Ask the Lord to order your steps (Ps. 37:23) so that you will not veer off the path he has set for you. And most of all, believe in your vision, yourself, and the God you serve to bring your vision to pass.

MY CONFESSION

I will seek God's direction for my life as I work toward the vision he's given me.

50

Develop a Giving Spirit

Opening the Door for Great Blessing

Give, and it will be given to you. A good measure, pressed down, shaken together and running over, will be poured into your lap. For with the measure you use, it will be measured to you.

LUKE 6:38

When I think of someone with a giving spirit, my good friend Pat immediately comes to mind. At that first Black Filmmaker Foundation meeting, I arrived late and nervously scanned the room for a seat. A kindhearted sister—Pat—smiled and pointed to a seat next to her. After the meeting, she and I formally introduced ourselves to each other, and I thanked her for rescuing me from embarrassment. We both got a good chuckle out of it.

As we stood there making small talk, several people greeted Pat, and I could tell she was a major influence in the group. As the room started to empty, she asked me to join some people going to a local restaurant to get a bite to eat. She didn't know me from Adam, but she eagerly welcomed me into her world.

Pat is known in entertainment circles for her humble and giving nature, her unselfishness, and her genuine happiness when others succeed. She's the first to pass along a résumé, make an introduction, call a contact, or volunteer her services for committees at work or mentorship opportunities for underprivileged youth—and always with a smile. Pat lives out 2 Corinthians 9:7: "Each man should give what he has decided in his heart to give, not reluctantly or under compulsion, for God loves a cheerful giver." She has a big heart and will help a stranger.

One evening at a Black History Month celebration, sponsored by Time Inc., I got the chance to see for myself how dearly loved Pat was. At the end of the program, the committee chairpersons were introducing the folks who had helped plan and coordinate the event. One by one, each person was introduced and thanked for his or her efforts. Each received hearty applause from the crowd of about two hundred. It seemed the announcer saved the best for last, because when Pat's name was called, she not only got thunderous applause, but she also got a standing ovation! I couldn't have been prouder. She deserved that praise and so much more.

POWER MOVE

Think about how you can become more of a giver. Is there a new intern at work who needs mentoring? A new mother who needs flexibility with her hours? The best giving opportunities are those that allow you to give of yourself—your time, your talents, and your spirit. Sometimes it's the little things that mean the most. Start where you are. Giving opens the way to receiving: "A generous man will himself be blessed, for he shares his food with the poor" (Prov. 22:9). But don't give just to get. Give because it's the right thing to do. People will notice if you have a hidden agenda. Make sure your heart is in the right place. "One man gives freely, yet gains even more; another withholds unduly, but comes to poverty. A generous man will prosper; he who refreshes others will himself be refreshed" (Prov. 11:24–25).

MY CONFESSION

I will open my arms to give, using Christ as my example.

51

When Racism Rears Its Ugly Head

Confronting Painful Situations with Grace

To show partiality is not good—yet a man
will do wrong for a piece of bread.

PROVERBS 28:21

Shortly after Barack Obama was elected as president of the United States, I heard a newscaster make a reference to "a post-racist America." I had to laugh. What country was he living in? And "post-racist" to whom? Certainly not to black people, I thought. As much as society would like to deny that racism still exists, despite our election of the first African American president, the truth is, racism finds ways to stay alive.

I'll never forget the first time I experienced racism on the job. I certainly didn't expect it. I had been recently hired at a local newspaper as a copywriter. It was my first "real" job where I could finally make use of my talents and hard-earned college degree. I was also the first African American in my department—the first since the newspaper's inception. My manager was a thirtysomething woman I immediately liked. One day, I was in her office with my co-worker Elaine (not her real name). I'm not sure how we got on the subject, but the issue of race and affirmative action came up. The details of the discussion are still fuzzy, but I remember the three of us laughing, and then my boss blurted out, "Oh, Carol, you were only hired because you're black."

The smile disappeared from my face, and a look of horror came across Elaine's face. I guess my boss caught herself, because she added, "And you're good." You could have cut the tension with a knife after that, so I excused myself. Minutes later, my boss came into my office and said, "I just want to apologize. Elaine pulled me aside and said my comment was probably very offensive to you. I apologize. I didn't mean it in a negative way."

I brushed it off, accepting her apology because I was newly hired and didn't want to make enemies right off the bat. But her comment caused me to think. Was that the way she really looked at me—as an affirmative action case? True, I was young with no real achievements under my belt yet, but did it not matter that I had a bachelor's degree in communications? That I was contributing writer for a book? That I was intelligent and a good employee? I guess none of those things mattered because her true feelings about me being hired had finally come out.

POWER MOVE

If you've ever encountered racism on the job, you know it's a hurtful, embarrassing, and painful experience. But it's a reality that African Americans and other people of color will endure at some point in their lives. One thing we must remember: our God is bigger than any racist on this planet. Let Christ dispel the darkness of that person's limited thinking, and continue to see yourself through his eyes—as an accomplished child of God.

MY CONFESSION

I will not repay evil with evil and will rejoice in the Lord's deliverance from racial prejudice.

52

Father Knows Best

When God Says No

Many are the plans in a man's heart, but
it is the LORD's purpose that prevails.

PROVERBS 19:21

I heard someone say that the Lord answers prayer with "yes," "no," or "wait." He never says "maybe" because then he'd be a wishy-washy God, not a God who does not change (Mal. 3:6). He has the goods; it's up to us to pray and believe we will receive what we ask for (Matt. 21:22). This is not to say that God will give us everything we ask for. Sometimes God will say no to our prayers for our own good. Maybe it's not his timing. Maybe our desires are covetous. Maybe we'll harm others if our prayer is answered right away because we lack maturity and wisdom. There can be a number of reasons why our every prayer isn't granted, but rest assured it's for our highest good. "We know that in all things God works for the good of those who love him, who have been called according to his purpose" (Rom. 8:28).

If you're a parent, you know full well that you can't give your children everything they ask for. Any good parent knows that some things his children ask for are frivolous, are selfishly motivated, or will ultimately destroy them. A slice of cake before dinner? The keys to the car at age fourteen? A $1,000 handbag? If we as earthly parents love our offspring enough not to overindulge them for their own sake, how much more would our heavenly Father, whose love we cannot fathom, not let us walk into a ditch? He has our ultimate well-being in mind—from the time we exit our mother's womb to the time we take our last breath on earth—and knows the path he's designed for our lives.

As I grow in Christ, my prayers become less "me-centric" and more "he-centric," as I learn to bend to whatever God's will is for my life. I'm not taking a passive stance by giving it all to God. I'm simply saying, "Lord, I'm tired of hitting my head against a wall trying to do things my way. I'm perfectly open to whatever you would have me do with this life you gave me." I'd rather be in his will than out of it.

Being out of God's will is a lonely, desperate place. The more you try to pry a door open, the more solid the seal—and you'll ruin your manicure!

POWER MOVE

The word *no* isn't always a bad thing. But what can be bad is our attitude about it. Commit today to embrace God's "no" and "wait" with gratitude for his love.

MY CONFESSION

Even when the Lord says "no," it's "yes" to my ultimate good.

53

A Prophet without Honor

Family and Friends May Doubt You, but God Never Does

Only in his hometown, among his relatives and in his own house is a prophet without honor.

MARK 6:4

You may be the lead soloist in your church choir. You may be a passionate Sunday school teacher whose class is filled to capacity every Sunday. You may be Employee of the Year on your job. Your accomplishments, however great or small, speak for themselves. You're a mover and shaker for God . . . but to family and friends, you're still someone's little girl. Don't worry, you're in excellent company. Jesus's family and friends said the same thing about him! "'Isn't this the carpenter? Isn't this Mary's son and the brother of James, Joseph, Judas and Simon? Aren't his sisters here with us?' And they took offense at him" (Mark 6:3). In the townspeople's eyes, he was only Jesus, the carpenter from "around the way," not the Savior and Son of God.

I remember when I got a promotion to editor from senior copywriter at work. It was the most exciting day of my career. This was a new career for me since most of my experience was in advertising, but it was one I was anxious to take on. Most of my co-workers were happy to see me make the switch and supported me fully. I had a fab going-away lunch and still cherish those memories.

Unfortunately, not all of my new co-workers were happy to see me come into their department. A select few wouldn't even speak to me, though I had tried repeatedly to make conversation. Being new to the job, I had a lot to learn, and the more allies I had, the better. The last thing I wanted to do was alienate the folks who could help me make the transition. But communication is a two-way street. I imagined that those who ignored me still saw me in a "lesser" role as copywriter, not as a peer or an equal. After a while, their coolness toward me didn't matter. I focused my energies on learning my new job and thanked God for the many who did help me.

POWER MOVE

It doesn't matter if your family, friends, or co-workers don't recognize your anointing. God gave you special gifts, talents, and desires, and he fully expects you to use them for his glory. The fact that you're excelling in any area is a testament to your obedience to do his will in your life. God wants his daughters to shine. "Let your light shine before men, that they may see your good deeds and praise your Father in heaven" (Matt. 5:16). Remember, Jesus had to leave his hometown because the people there could see him only one way and couldn't receive or accept his message of forgiveness and salvation. But people's lack of acceptance didn't stop Jesus's ministry, which continues to this day. Don't let it stop yours!

MY CONFESSION

I will not shrink because people want me to. I will shine because God wants me to!

54

Exceed Your Reach

Go the Extra Mile and Experience Greater Blessings

He who works his land will have abundant food,
but he who chases fantasies lacks judgment.

Proverbs 12:11

You've heard the phrase "go the extra mile." I'm pretty sure it originated with Jesus, when he told his disciples, "If someone forces you to go one mile, go with him two miles" (Matt. 5:41). He encouraged them to go beyond what they were asked to do—to exceed their reach. Are you exceeding your reach at work? Or are you barely getting by, doing exactly what is required of you and no more?

One of my former assistants, Diane, made a habit of exceeding her reach. She came early to work, not because I asked, but because a few extra minutes in the morning gave her time to be on top of things before the phone began to ring. When she was done with the work on her desk, she didn't play computer solitaire; she came to see me and asked what else she could do. Guess what? When it was time for her review, I made special note of her initiative.

Even God goes the extra mile when it comes to us: "Now unto him that is able to do exceeding abundantly above all that we ask or think, according to the power that worketh in us" (Eph. 3:20 KJV). We may ask him for knowledge, and he in his loving-kindness will give us knowledge *and* wisdom—more than we asked for!

POWER MOVE

If your boss asks you to do a task, take it to the next level—do what she asks plus a task she didn't ask you to do—and see what happens. My bet is that she'll be impressed you took the initiative to do something that needed to be done. Just be sure to do the initial task well so that she feels confident you can do more. If you don't do the small task well, she won't trust you with larger assignments.

MY CONFESSION

I will do "exceeding abundantly" more than is asked of me in every area of my life.

55

On-the-Job Moms

Fostering Independence in Your Kids

Train a child in the way he should go, and
when he is old he will not turn from it.

Proverbs 22:6

Some moms work because they want to, and some moms work because they have to. Whichever category you fall into, know that with prayer, planning, and discipline, you can successfully work and have a family. This isn't the easiest option, but it doesn't have to be a negative situation for your children. If you're a working mom, you can teach your children important life skills that are harder for them to learn if you're home with them. As mothers, sometimes we're prone to do things for our kids that they can easily do for themselves. We're nurturers, so our first instinct is to wait on them hand and foot. For example, for years I did all of the family's laundry on weekends—loads of it. But when I started to travel on business, I was away on weekends and couldn't do the laundry. So the simple solution was to show the kids how to wash and iron their own clothes. And they've been doing it ever since.

Our first ministry is to our family, and that's the way God intended it to be. But he's not blind—he knows our challenges as single moms, working moms, and career moms. Our kids aren't destined for reform school just because we aren't at home to supervise their every move. We can train them to be strong, levelheaded, and independent thinkers. Here are a few ways:

- **Give them regular chores.** When each of my boys turned eight years old, I taught them how to wash dishes (whether I had a dishwasher or not), including how to keep the water at the right temperature so they didn't get scalded, how to apply the right amount of dish detergent to the sponge, how not to cut themselves when washing goblets. Did they make mistakes? Absolutely—at first. But eventually they didn't anymore, and my kitchen was clean when I came home after a long day at work.

  When the boys turned thirteen, I taught them how to clean the bathroom (I needed more patience here). I'd usually have to go over it and show them where they missed a spot, but this was another chore off my already full plate. I didn't have the money to hire a housekeeper back then, so we all had to pitch in.
- **Give them clear directions.** As the boys got into their early teen years, I could trust them to stay in the house by themselves, but not without instructions: "Do not let anyone in the house when Dad and I are not home." "Do not turn on the stove and walk away." "Do not run up my phone bill" (this was before all-inclusive plans). "Do not go outside for any reason other than a fire."

  To this day we joke about the time I came home to find my youngest son David at the stove with a chair nearby. I had instructed him never to put anything on the stove and walk away, so that boy had pulled up a kitchen chair right next to the stove, just in case he got tired while monitoring the pot!

- **Give them a break.** No matter how much responsibility we give them, kids are not adults and won't behave like adults. They're still kids and need to have fun. You're the parent and it's ultimately up to you, but I think you should cut them some slack on the weekend if they're on top of things during the week. We all need a release from the pressures of life. If they want to stay out a little later or play video games an extra hour, let them. If they're good, obedient kids, this could be your nonverbal way of communicating how much you appreciate them for being a team player while you're out earning a living for the family. (Rub it in if you need to, just to remind them!)

POWER MOVE

Make a list of the things you're most worried about if you go back to work. If you're already working, make a list of the things you're worried about for the coming year regarding your children. (Each age group has different needs. Teenagers need more monitoring since they have more freedom than, say, a five-year-old.) Then talk with other working moms, your mom, or your friends, or read a good parenting book. Create specific plans to combat your worries.

MY CONFESSION

I will enlist my children's help and stress the importance of teamwork in our family.

56

Never Remain Neutral

Take a Stand and Stick to It

So, because you are lukewarm—neither hot nor cold—I am about to spit you out of my mouth.

Revelation 3:16

I once heard a publicist say that the best radio and TV guests are those with strong opinions. You won't catch them sitting on any fence. They stand up for what they believe in, whether others agree with it or not, and don't change their minds at the drop of a hat. Usually these folks' viewpoints are so strong, they may at one time or another put their foot in their mouth. People who take a stand often do. You're not always going to like these folks, but you probably will remember them.

Imagine if Jesus were a "why can't everybody just get along?" type of guy. Where would we be? If he were that type of Savior (thank God he wasn't!), we wouldn't have salvation or the forgiveness of sins. He would have been so busy trying to please the Pharisees, the Roman rulers, and everyone else that he would not have pleased the one who sent him in the first place: God.

But Jesus did take a stand, and he showed us how to do that with love, kindness, and compassion. And when it came to sin and the hypocrisy of the Pharisees, Jesus was hard on them because he knew their hearts were evil. He called them out and didn't hold back. "Woe to you, teachers of the law and Pharisees, you hypocrites! You shut the kingdom of heaven in men's faces. You yourselves do not enter, nor will you let those enter who are trying to" (Matt. 23:13). They tried everything they could to get on his nerves and to deter him from his ministry by tempting him (Matt. 16:1), demanding to see a sign (Matt. 12:38–39), trying to trap him (Matt. 22:15), and plotting to kill him (Matt. 12:14). But with all of that opposition, Jesus's message did not change; his love did not change; he did not change. He took a stand and did not waver—even upon the cross.

The Lord admonishes you to "be strong and very courageous" (Josh. 1:7). When you stand up for what's fair, right, and just, he is with you. It doesn't matter what your boss or co-workers think. Stick to your guns. You and the Lord are a majority!

POWER MOVE

How do you think you are perceived? As someone who is committed to her faith, her values, and her opinions, or someone who is double-minded (James 1:8) and unable to take a firm stand? Standing by your beliefs does not mean you have to be arrogant or obnoxious. Jesus was neither, and he drew thousands to him during his earthly ministry.

MY CONFESSION

Lord, give me the strength to stand by my beliefs, principles, and values as I stand up for you.

57

Keep It Real

Showing Your Vulnerability Will Strengthen Your Witness

Jesus wept.

John 11:35

Maybe you've asked someone, "Read any good books lately?" and they huff, "I only read the Bible." Or you ask, "How are you?" and they assure you they are "blessed and highly favored." Now, there's nothing wrong with those answers, but they limit others' perceptions of you. Christians, just like everyone else, get tired, are disappointed, feel insecure, and face temptation. But some of us are so bent on showing the world that we are "set apart" that we cannot connect with people who might otherwise listen to the Good News of Christ.

One of the reasons the Pharisees hated Jesus so much was because he showed his human side and wasn't pompous like they were. He called them out on their twisted theology (Matt. 23:23), and they accused him of carousing with tax collectors and "sinners" (Matt. 9:11). But don't you love Jesus's response? "It is not the healthy who need a doctor, but the sick" (v. 12).

If the "sinners" at Matthew's house didn't feel comfortable around Jesus, they probably would have left before dinner. But there was something about Jesus that drew them. He got so angry at the moneychangers who were dealing in the temple that he threw the tables down (Matt. 21:12–13), but right after that he healed the lame and sick (v. 14). Overwhelmingly, though, it was his love, his honesty, and his compassion that compelled them. I'd imagine that after the dinner, when these same "sinners" were exiting Matthew's home, they'd say, "That Jesus is alright with me. I'm going to his meeting tomorrow by the Sea of Galilee."

Let's follow the Lord's lead and let our lives speak for our Christian walk.

POWER MOVE

Are you isolated from everyone else at work? Do others perceive you as being "holier than thou"? Do nonbelievers prefer not to have lunch with you? If so, make an effort to get to know at least one person and become an ally to him or her. Maybe you and another person work on projects together or report to the same boss. Volunteer to help that person with an assignment. Just because someone doesn't know Christ doesn't mean that they're "evil." Chances are, they have more in common with you than you think. Stay prayerful, and the Lord will open a door for you to impact the world for him.

MY CONFESSION

I will, above all, be myself and be approachable, just as Jesus was.

58

Just Do It

Waiting and Procrastinating Aren't the Same Thing

The sluggard craves and gets nothing, but the desires of the diligent are fully satisfied.

Proverbs 13:4

I saw this quote by Dame Flora Robson in a copy of *Guideposts* magazine: "Ask God's blessing on your work, but do not also ask him to do it." So many of us want to do great things for God, but for some reason we just can't get ourselves going. How many projects have we put off? How many ideas have we talked ourselves out of? How many dreams have we shelved, telling ourselves we'll get to them after the kids are older, after we turn forty, after we get enough money, after we retire? Somehow we think it will get easier—or maybe we're waiting for God to do the heavy lifting on our dreams.

I had set a goal to become editor-in-chief shortly after I became editor. I knew there were at least two steps between those two jobs, but I decided editor-in-chief was the title that held the most weight, and that's the title I wanted. About two years after I became editor, I got promoted to senior editor. After more hard work and determination, I finally received the promotion I wanted and deserved: editor-in-chief! Did I ask God for a promotion? Yes. But I knew I had to do the work. He wasn't going to bless me with a position he knew I didn't deserve. God provided all I needed—but he did expect me to participate in my dream!

We live in a fast-paced society where everything is due *yesterday*. Physicians overbook their office hours so they can see as many of their patients as possible. Executives hold conference calls so they can save time. Deadlines rule most of our lives. Time to take out the trash. Time to take the kids to school. Time to catch the bus. We always find time to do the things we *have* to do. But what about the things we *want* to do? Time waits for no one, so whatever dream, vision, idea, or plan God has given you, just do it. Now is the time!

POWER MOVE

My former pastor used to say that the best ideas were in the cemetery—buried along with the people who had dreams they never acted upon. What are your plans, goals, and dreams? Write them down. Give yourself a timetable so you'll stay on track. Buddy up with a friend or someone else who is committed to a goal so you can keep each other accountable. God's not going to write your business plan, set up customer meetings, or make a demo tape for you. You have to do it yourself. He will bless the work of your hands so you'll be encouraged to continue.

MY CONFESSION

I will make the most of every day, for time waits for no one!

59

Sexual Harassment on the Job

Adopt a Zero-Tolerance Policy for Workplace Abuse

Flee from sexual immorality. All other sins a man commits are outside his body, but he who sins sexually sins against his own body.

1 Corinthians 6:18

There's nothing more humiliating than being sexually harassed on your job. It starts with a lingering look. A roving of his eyes over your body in a suggestive way. Then he'll sneak up on you, invading your space. When he speaks to you, he gets a little too close. You don't like this kind of attention and it's unwarranted, but you don't know what to do about it. The man may be in a position of power, and you feel your job will be threatened if you tell someone. You don't want to tell your husband or boyfriend because then you know there *will* be trouble—no doubt about it. But you must do something because he's coming on stronger and his advances are more aggressive.

As a Christian woman, first ask God for guidance. Some situations may be more volatile than others, especially if you work in a male-dominated industry or business. But God is a just judge and will not allow perpetrators to go free, "for he guards the course of the just and protects the way of his faithful ones" (Prov. 2:8).

I'll never forget the time I was sexually harassed on the job. My co-worker Elaine (not her real name) and I had gone to meet with an advertising executive regarding a sales promotion for his department. This man was nice enough, cordial, and had about two hundred people on his staff. As we were sitting in his office, we noticed that he sat way back in his chair and began staring at both of us. Then out of the blue, he asked, "Ladies, if your stomach was really hurting, what would you do?" Puzzled, we muttered that we'd take Pepto Bismol, maybe lie down, those types of answers.

Looking slightly annoyed, he said, "No, I mean what would you *do*? Show me." Elaine and I looked at each other like this guy was nuts. Still, Elaine doubled over in her chair, pretending to be writhing in pain. He then looked at me, and I followed suit. But I had noticed, to my horror and disgust, that Mr. Ad Man had put his hands down his pants as we were bent over, playing out his sick "stomachache" fantasy. Now, mind you, this happened in February and we weren't in skimpy clothing, so he certainly wasn't reacting to our dress code.

On our way back to our offices, I asked Elaine, "Did you see what I saw?"

"I sure did," she replied.

Minutes later we were in our manager's office, retelling the whole episode. Human resources paid us a visit the next day, followed by senior management. Come to find out, this guy had molested dozens of the mostly female workers in his department over the last thirteen years. All of them had been too frightened to blow the whistle on him, so they either suffered in silence or found another job. The human resources manager at the time confided in me that he had literally cried when one of the women told what had happened to her. God used the incident with Elaine and me to put a stop to that man's abuse.

POWER MOVE

If you are put in a situation where you do not feel comfortable, you have to speak up. There are stricter laws in place now than there were in the early nineties, when this happened to me. Tell your manager or human resources manager immediately. No one should be harassed during working hours for any reason. Ask God to intervene and he will.

MY CONFESSION

I will not tolerate abuse of any kind from my superiors and will report it at once. God is on my side.

60

Deciding to Stay Home with Your Kids

Banish the Guilt and Embrace the Blessing

Her children arise and call her blessed.

PROVERBS 31:28

Working mothers have a hard enough time juggling home and work without the added pressure of society telling them what they should or should not do. "Stay home with the kids; they need you the most," some say. "You shouldn't have to abandon your career because you have a family," others will argue. But staying home is a decision that a woman must make on her own or along with her spouse. It will affect the children, the parents, and the household financial picture, so everyone needs to be in one accord.

A publishing colleague of mine was trying to decide whether to stay at home with her one-year-old daughter. Her husband made a great living and had been bugging her for months to make a decision. He told her he had her back financially for all the little "extras" (handbags, in her case!) that she may crave. Not long after we were discussing this over lunch, I got an email saying she'd made the plunge.

They'd waited a couple years to have this baby and wanted to enjoy her.

Some women are fortunate enough that money is not a factor in their decision to stay home with their kids. Other couples struggle with the issue—they aren't comfortable financially and know that a single income will be a strain. But the children are well worth it. Then there are women who marry late in life and decide to have a baby after a successful career and financial stability.

Whichever category you fall into, know that the end result—you being home with your children—is your choice to make. If you decide to stay at home, don't let messages from others guilt you.

POWER MOVE

Life at home with the kids is a lot of work, but it has its rewards as well. No rushing home after work. No using up vacation days for play dates and doctor visits. Staying at home with a toddler is time-consuming and tiresome, but the time you have with your child is worth every messy moment. You can get another job; you can't get back the years you miss with your child.

MY CONFESSION

My decision to stay at home with my child will be a blessing, as children are a blessing from God.

61

Turn Your Back on the Crowd

Focus on Your Goals and Leave the Naysayers Behind

> I press on toward the goal to win the
> prize for which God has called me
> heavenward in Christ Jesus.
>
> PHILIPPIANS 3:14

We've become so fixated on other people's lives that we've forgotten our own dreams and goals. As a matter of fact, most folks don't even have dreams or goals. They have wishes. "I wish I were rich." "I wish I were skinny." "I wish I had a husband." Wishes don't create legacies—goals and dreams do! If God has given you a special dream or plan for your life, you may have to leave the crowd behind. Unlike wishes, goals require time. Don't expect people to understand why you can't go to the movies or get together. They'll probably resent you for it. "Who does she think she is? She thinks she's better than us?" the petty ones will say. Others will operate on a more passive-aggressive level—they're happy for you, but . . . "Do you really think you're going to start a business with no money?"

You will know who your friends are—and aren't—when you attempt something that will require great faith, great sacrifice, and a huge amount of time. Those girlfriends who truly love you and support you (I call them "ride-or-die chicks") are with you every step of the way—praying for you, keeping the children while you have meetings, treating you to a manicure (Lord knows you haven't had time to get to the salon!). If you have friends like that, thank God for them.

Then there are those who want to deter you from your business. They'll call you to talk about nothing in particular, just to kill time. They don't ask how your project is coming along because they don't really want to know. Or, if they do ask, it's usually, "You still working on that thing?"

In order to effect positive change and achieve your goals, something will have to give. It shouldn't be your job—if you're working nine to five, you must go to work until your dream comes to fruition. It shouldn't be church—you need the spiritual fuel and Christian fellowship to get you through the days when you want to give up. So the only thing left is your social life, and that usually takes the biggest hit. Those with nothing to do, who read all the celebrity tabloids and envy the designer handbags and mansions, will love to pick apart your plans and dreams.

It's easy to *say* you want all the trappings of success—big houses, fancy cars, and money in the bank—but it's hard to put the time, energy, or sacrifice into making it happen. Dreams don't come true overnight. They take hard work, dedication, perseverance, and sealing your ears to negative words. "Lazy hands make a man poor, but diligent hands bring wealth" (Prov. 10:4). Keep your distance from those who don't support you fully. You'll be glad you did.

POWER MOVE

Who supports your dreams? List three people you can count on for support, and make plans to be in touch with them every week. Can't list three? Commit to finding new friends who will lift you up.

MY CONFESSION

I will turn my back on the crowd of naysayers who would try to deter me from my goals.

62

Go Ye!

Discipleship Is Key On the Job and Off

He said to them, "Go into all the world and preach the good news to all creation."

Mark 16:15

Jesus and the Pharisees could not have been more different. Jesus went where the people were—weddings (John 2:1–2), synagogues (Matt. 12:9), houses of rulers (Mark 5:38–42)—but mostly he took to the streets (Matt. 4:23). He even went to dine with tax collectors and "sinners" at Levi's house (Mark 2:15). He knew some people would not come to him, so he had to go to them. The Pharisees and teachers of the law bitterly criticized Jesus for this because they did not mingle with everyday folk. They were "religious" leaders and felt certain people were beneath them.

Keeping Jesus in the mix on the job doesn't mean it's the only place we preach the good news. I think Jesus talked about things wherever people were most receptive. In our day people buy groceries, they work out, and they get their hair done on Saturday mornings, so those places are great mission fields. Don't be afraid to venture into unknown territory. You have the Holy Spirit on your side.

Years ago, my husband and I took evangelism classes on how to witness to various demographics and ethnic groups. What we learned is that we cannot effectively minister to everyone the same way. We have to speak their language without patronizing them. The insight and knowledge we gained was worth every hour spent. If your church offers a class on evangelism, take it. Or find another church or Christian organization that offers the class so you can be "a workman who does not need to be ashamed and who correctly handles the word of truth" (2 Tim. 2:15).

POWER MOVE

Ask God to help you be receptive to the needs around you as you go about your day. Who needs a word of encouragement? A prayer? Keep yourself open to where God can use you today.

MY CONFESSION

I will witness to unbelievers wherever I am and whenever the Lord presents an opportunity.

63

Build Bridges, Not Walls

Finding Kindred Spirits

Two are better than one, because they
have a good return for their work.

ECCLESIASTES 4:9

For most of my working life, I've been the one and only African American among my co-workers. I worked at a popular boutique in midtown Manhattan on Saturdays, starting when I was sixteen up until the week I left for college. Even though I was the only black girl, I wasn't intimidated. I made friends easily with the other teen girls, and we shared our dreams of going to college—and of boys! Oddly enough, about ten years later, it happened again: I was hired into a department that had never had any African Americans. I didn't know it at the time, but apparently shortly before I arrived, others in executive positions had put pressure on the management of that department to hire an African American. Still, I had a new opportunity—my first "real" job—and nothing was going to rain on my parade. Although I didn't know anyone, I was a people person, and my new co-workers made me feel welcome.

Over time, my co-workers and I became like a little family and saw each other through good times and bad. We visited each other's homes, attended baby showers, celebrated birthdays, and bid each other tearful good-byes as we each left the company. Most of us are still friends to this day. So I consider myself blessed. Some of my African American friends and colleagues have relayed work horror stories—from not being invited to important meetings to being overlooked for well-deserved promotions to having their personal lives called into question. So the isolation, the neglect, and the lack of inclusiveness are real issues, especially among professional blacks. But even if you're the "one and only," you can still find people, regardless of race, who will work with you, not against you.

No matter what, God can move on your behalf when you don't even know he's moving. If you keep your heart and mind open, he will help you find kindred spirits. Don't limit yourself because you're the "one and only" in your place of business. Chances are, you and your co-workers have more in common than you know. But you have to give them a chance. Regardless of what society says, we're all equal in God's sight.

POWER MOVE

If you're the only African American in your office, reach out to your co-workers, even if they don't make the first move. People are people, and there's good and bad in everyone, regardless of race. The light of God is irresistible. Whoever sees the light of Christ in you will gravitate toward you, regardless of your skin color. Remember, you're there for a reason!

MY CONFESSION

I will allow God to use me on the job, and I will reach out to my co-workers regardless of race.

64

Let Me Upgrade You!

God Wants to Promote You and Elevate You to New Heights

For promotion cometh neither from the east, nor from the west, nor from the south. But God is the judge: he putteth down one, and setteth up another.

Psalm 75:6–7 KJV

We all like to be upgraded. On an airline, to be upgraded from coach to business class is a big deal. The seats are cushy and make for a more comfortable trip, your flight attendant dotes on you, and the food . . . well, you actually get food! At the car rental, an upgrade means a roomier, fancier, and fully loaded car.

God is also in the upgrade business. He doesn't want us to stay where we are. He wants us to learn, grow, and be in positions of influence and authority. The more Christians there are in influential places, the better position we're in to mentor others, show Christ's love, and manage with integrity. God wants us to expand our knowledge, apply that knowledge, and move to the next level. If you are prepared, ready, and willing, God can—and will—move on your behalf. He's not going to set you up for failure. He wants you to succeed, like any good parent would. But you have to have your stuff together. If you're not ready, he'll wait until you are.

My father-in-law, Larry, is a prime example of God's promotion. For years he worked for a large energy delivery company as a mechanic in the garages where the delivery trucks were maintained. Though he was not formally educated, his strong work ethic and masterful skills got him promoted to supervisor. He managed a couple dozen mechanics in that garage, and his department was responsible for making sure the garages and trucks were properly maintained. His job as supervisor was more administrative and managerial. He could have easily turned down that promotion—he's a hands-on guy and liked "getting dirty"—and forfeited the experience, the money, and the chance for real ministry, but he didn't. As a result, he managed to support a wife, eight children, and a sickly mother-in-law all on one salary.

Larry also showed his staff what it meant to be a team player. For example, when one of the guys came in sick and was still trying his best to work on a truck one wintry morning, Larry left the warmth of his office, pulled on a pair of overalls, and told the guy to go home. He would finish up on the truck. He would do many things like that over the years, including praying over every meal he ordered in when they pulled all-nighters. But more than that, he was able to witness to his men about Christ. He even invited one particular young man to his church who later accepted Christ and became active in the ministry.

My father-in-law allowed the Lord to upgrade him. How about you?

POWER MOVE

Think about your current job. Now imagine how much more you could accomplish by moving to the next level. Think about the money. The higher your salary, the more you can tithe and give to the ministry, the more you can give to charity, the more you can bless your family. Think about the possibilities of a promotion—of improving your life, expanding your skill set, getting new work experience, and being Jesus's representative on all fronts in business.

MY CONFESSION

I know that promotions are often God-given. I will prepare myself so that when the Lord calls, I will be ready to move.

65

Let Go and Let God

Don't Let Unforgiveness Block Your Blessings

Get rid of all bitterness, rage and anger, brawling and slander, along with every form of malice. Be kind and compassionate to one another, forgiving each other, just as in Christ God forgave you.

Ephesians 4:31–32

I'm sure you've heard the cliché, "Time heals all wounds." Sometimes that's true and sometimes it isn't. We all have experienced someone or something that has hurt us and caused seemingly irreparable damage. Whether the offense happened years ago or last week, the pain of the past seems to go on forever. And even though the Lord commands us to forgive, we may still struggle with unforgiveness. But the truth of the matter is, unless we find it in our hearts to forgive, God won't forgive us our sins (Matt. 6:15). And that will hinder our blessings for sure, since God is in the blessing business!

You may have been passed up for a promotion (again) as you watched the new employee you trained step into the spot. Or a friend could have betrayed a confidence at work and ruined your credibility with your boss. Or your husband could have cheated on you with another woman. There could be a multitude of scenarios. But the important thing is to realize that none of us is perfect. We've all sinned and fallen short of the glory of God (Romans 3:23). I've hurt people. You've hurt people. We all have. So if the Lord can forgive us our trespasses, we can forgive others.

Forgiving is not an easy thing to do, and it won't happen overnight. Depending on what happened, it may take a while for you to heal. But what you don't want is to let your bitterness and unforgiveness hamper your prayers or your blessings. Pray for that insecure co-worker, that tyrannical boss, or that straying husband. "When you stand praying, if you hold anything against anyone, forgive him, so that your Father in heaven may forgive you your sins" (Mark 11:25).

POWER MOVE

We all have harbored unforgiveness toward someone at one time or another. It's not a good feeling. You get angry all over again just thinking about what that person did to you. You sincerely want to forgive them, and in time you may. But as the saying goes, "Resentment is like drinking poison and waiting for the other person to die." Unforgiveness and bitterness can eat you alive and stymie your spiritual growth. So take this day, this second, and think about someone who has wronged you. Say a prayer for that person and ask God to come into their heart. You have too much to accomplish for the Lord, for your family, and on your job to allow the enemy to block your blessings!

MY CONFESSION

I release my enemies in Jesus's name and will forgive them as Christ forgives me.

66

When Work, Church, and Home Collide

How to Manage Conflicts and Set Priorities

The mouth of the righteous man utters wisdom, and his tongue speaks what is just.

Psalm 37:30

You can have too much of a good thing, even when that good thing is church. So many Christian women find it hard to juggle church activities, demanding work schedules, and home responsibilities. We're in an age where we want to do it all, but often that leads only to feeling fatigued, worn-out, and resentful because we can't be everything to everyone. If you must work late on the night you teach Bible study, that's a problem. If your husband has planned a romantic dinner date the night you promised to visit the sick and shut-in members of your church with your pastor, that can cause strife in your marriage.

Remember, just because the church is asking doesn't mean God is asking. We need to be wise stewards of our time. We need to remember that people, not programs, are what matter most to God.

When I was a leader in my church, I had to make the tough decision to step down. This was difficult because I loved the ministry. But I loved my family more. Being at church four days out of the workweek put a serious strain on my family life. The kids weren't getting their homework done because we had to be at church by six or seven at night. They'd be sleepy and irritable by the time we did come home late at night and couldn't concentrate. I would come home after a hard day's work and be annoyed and frustrated too, but more at myself for allowing others to dictate my time. So I had to put my foot down. No more weeknights at church except for Bible study, which was once a week. My first ministry was to my family, and if I couldn't manage the affairs of my home properly, God certainly wouldn't trust me with anything else.

It was the best decision I made. The kids' grades were back on par because they were well rested and alert for school. I had time to cook full meals and help the boys with their homework and school projects. Our family was back on track. I'm quite sure the Lord didn't hold my decision not to attend weeknight services against me.

POWER MOVE

If the question to take on a project came at work instead of church, one of the things you would do is look at the "opportunity cost"—if you say yes to the project, would it direct resources away from a better opportunity? The next time you're feeling pulled in too many directions, take a look at the cost of the opportunity before you respond.

MY CONFESSION

I will ask for God's help in discerning the best ways to spend my time.

67

Know When It's Time to Go

If You've Outgrown Your Position, God Will Move You On

Show me your ways, O Lord, teach me
your paths; guide me in your truth and
teach me, for you are God my Savior,
and my hope is in you all day long.

Psalm 25:4–5

Sometimes we are stubborn and resistant to the leading of the Holy Spirit. When we have outgrown a position or God has another project or plan for our lives, he will often close doors in the job we currently have. Nothing seems to bring us joy, projects don't go as planned, we don't get the raise that seemed inevitable. If things are going wrong when they should be going right, stop to seek God's direction. Is he closing one door so he can open another someplace else? Perhaps there is a better job, a new career path, or a new position in your company. But you won't know what blessing lies ahead if you're still stuck in your old position.

I have a friend who experienced this firsthand. She was an intelligent marketing executive who'd helped build and shape one of her company's divisions from the ground up. But over the years, management changed hands—her beloved and trusted boss had gotten the ax, and she had a new boss who didn't know her or respect her contributions. She was overlooked at meetings, important information never trickled down to her, and this boss had a new "second chair." Once a rising marketing star, my friend now felt isolated and alone. She was miserable and wanted out. But God had other plans for her.

On a whim, she went to a meeting a leading cosmetics company was holding. She signed on as a consultant just to make a few extra bucks and get her mind off her workplace woes. Three years later, she was a regional director in that company! Before long, she'd forgotten all about her inattentive boss and basked in the glory of her new business.

After she gave birth to her second child, she knew it was time to leave her main job. She had her husband's support and stepped out in faith to pursue a career that made her feel valued, gave her time with her family, and allowed her to make her own hours. God allowed her to become uncomfortable because he had something better in store for her.

Be receptive to the Holy Spirit, be obedient, and know that God is with you always. All you have to do is trust him and have faith.

POWER MOVE

Do you feel "shut down" in your present position? Take a look at the facts. Have you done your best work? Did the environment change, or did you? Sometimes we've achieved all we were meant to achieve in a position. Look for new opportunities for growth and trust God to place you where you belong.

MY CONFESSION

I will look for open doors, not stare at closed ones.

68

My Soul Says Yes

How to Develop a Willing Spirit

"If you are willing and obedient, you will eat the best from the land; but if you resist and rebel, you will be devoured by the sword." For the mouth of the LORD has spoken.

ISAIAH 1:19–20

If your work is like mine, you know that in order to actually get things done, everyone has to give a little more than the job description implies. Extra copies need to be made, procedures need to be explained to new employees, or another set of eyes is needed on a project. These are the unspoken expectations of a workplace—but if you neglect them, you'll hear plenty. And that rebellious spirit has a way of following you to places like your salary review or your promotion plans, or just when you need an extra pair of hands yourself.

Sometimes we hinder our blessings at work because we dig in our heels and aren't willing to do the little extras that will make us stand out and ultimately help us get ahead. The Bible says that if we show willingness and obedience, which go hand in hand, we will eat the best from the land (all the good things the job provides).

My dad is a prime example of this biblical principle. Neither one of my parents was formally educated. As a matter of fact, Dad barely completed the seventh grade. He had to quit school to work and help support the family. But he developed a strong work ethic before he even realized he had one.

I remember as a young girl when Dad and my uncle Rob would go fishing in Montauk Point, the southernmost part of Long Island, New York. Back then we lived in the South Bronx, and it was about a three-hour drive to Montauk Point. Mom would pack a hearty box lunch of fried chicken, Wonder bread, boiled eggs, and a six-pack of sodas for their trip. She knew Dad would come home exhausted from being on the water all day long.

Sure enough, he'd come home the next afternoon, sweaty and tired, with an ice chest full of porgies, bluefish, and trout. Everyone in our housing project knew that when Mr. Hill went fishing, there was a good chance their own freezers would be full. Dad always had compassion for the single mothers in the building and tried to lend a hand whenever he could. He had daughters their age and felt a paternal instinct toward them.

One neighbor, a thirtysomething woman with four kids, came down to visit Mom, and Dad was in the middle of cleaning the fish. She remarked how she had a taste for some fish, and of course Dad dug into the cooler, scooped out about six or seven large fish, and put them in a plastic bag for her. "Here, take some for you and the kids," he said. She held up the bag, knowing the fish hadn't been cleaned or scaled yet. Dad sensed she didn't know how to clean fish and offered to do it for her.

My mother and I exchanged looks. We both knew Dad would not only give people fish, he'd clean them, scale them, and package them in freezer paper if it took him all night—and sometimes it did.

No matter how late he had to stay up, how tired he was, or how cold his dinner got, if he was helping someone, my dad was totally committed—willing, ready, and able to go above and beyond what was asked or expected of him. At ninety-three, he's still blessed with good health and devoted children, grandchildren, great-grandchildren, and great-great-grandchildren (we're a productive bunch!). I believe Dad's willing spirit gave him favor with the Lord and was the reason we never saw a hungry day in our lives (Ps. 37:25).

If we develop a willing spirit, we'll say yes to the opportunities that God wants to bless us with, and we will succeed in all we do.

POWER MOVE

Today, look for genuine ways to say yes. You don't have to be willing to do everything, but find extra ways to help with the common goals you all have at work.

MY CONFESSION

I will be as willing as possible to help where needed.

69

Wise Counsel

Why Mentors Are Important at Every Level

Plans fail for lack of counsel, but with
many advisers they succeed.

PROVERBS 15:22

None of us gets where we are by ourselves. The most successful people I know have mentors—people who freely give of themselves and their time to lead, guide, and advise on career moves. The Bible encourages mentors and admonishes us not to lean on our own understanding. You don't have to have a corporate career to have a mentor. If you are serious about your profession, ask God to send people into your life to help you. Those people are one of the gifts God gives us by putting us within a community.

I consider myself incredibly blessed to have wonderful mentors who have given selflessly of their time and expertise over the course of several years. I met Terrie Williams while she was vice president of publicity at *Essence* magazine—at age thirty-five, the youngest vice president the magazine had ever had. It was 1987, and I was eight months pregnant with my youngest son. I had sent Terrie a résumé and letter, expressing interest in a freelance position in her department.

She called me back a week after I'd sent the letter to say that unfortunately she didn't have any positions available, but she would keep my résumé on file. I never forgot that moment. Most execs are too busy for personal phone calls, but Terrie took the time.

That was over twenty years ago, and I can still depend on Terrie for sound advice, encouragement, and support to this day. Over the years, she became a renowned and respected celebrity publicist with A-list clients in entertainment, sports, and business.

Another invaluable mentor for me has been Henry McGee. My friend Pat introduced him to me in the mid-nineties while I was considering a job in the cable industry. I met with Henry for advice on re-careering and was impressed by his willingness to help me. (He even critiqued my résumé, which he good-naturedly pointed out lacked subject-verb agreement. I immediately fixed it!) Although Henry is the president of HBO Video and travels all over the globe on business, he still makes time to advise me on my career and other business matters.

Both Henry and Terrie have been instrumental in my professional growth, and I've learned so much from them over the years. I value their opinions, trust their judgment, and cherish their friendship.

POWER MOVE

Most people will help you if they know you're serious about your career. Executives and influential people have busy schedules and can't afford to waste time. If they sense you're "jive," you won't get a call back. Be serious, be prepared, and be on time! I know from experience that a half hour is a lot of time when a person's schedule is chock-full of meetings, deadlines, and business lunches and dinners. So be sensitive to time limitations when you ask for a meeting. Look inside and outside your profession for good mentors. Do you know anyone who has navigated their life well, not just their career? Set up a meeting with them this month.

MY CONFESSION

I will look for good advice to help me succeed.

70

How a Shepherd Leads

Managing People Is Never Easy

Then I will give you shepherds after
my own heart, who will lead you with
knowledge and understanding.

JEREMIAH 3:15

If you supervise people, you know how difficult it can be. Besides managing the day-to-day responsibilities of the job, you also have to manage personalities—which can range from passive to strong-willed to drama queens (and kings).

As Christians, we have the greatest boss on our side to lead and guide us as we lead and guide others. Some workers will be a dream; others will be a nightmare. It's up to us to use the wisdom of God and the Word of God to manage all personality types successfully through prayer, intercession, and common sense.

Some of the people you manage will be "sheep" (teachable and easy to manage) and others will be "goats" (stubborn, negative, and strong-willed). But they are all God's children, and when we don't treat them with the respect of a creation of God, all manner of trouble begins. My best managing has happened when I separated who a person is (God's creation) from what he or she did. In other words, all people are accepted; all actions are not. Have I made mistakes while leading? Absolutely. Being a boss is never easy, and there is a learning (and experience) curve. With headship comes responsibility.

God has entrusted you to be a leader to your staff, and he expects you to lead with kindness, compassion, and a sense of fairness. Whether you're listening to a complaint, solving a crisis, or managing expectations, keep the focus on what was done or what needs to be done. The truth is, you can never fully understand the motives of another, and you can rarely change those motives. Set an example of respect and service with your staff, and expect them to do the same.

POWER MOVE

If you're a parent, you know that no two children are the same, but you love them anyway. Similarly, some staff members will be more high-maintenance and need more attention, more guidance, and more praise than others. Then there are the self-starters who are proactive, responsive, and eager to learn. You have to be the boss to the "sheep" and the "goats," and you have to be fair to both, so look at the Gospels for the way Jesus led. What can you apply to your own situation today?

MY CONFESSION

I will thank God for the opportunity to lead others.

71

Ready When You Are!

The Lord Is Ready to Bless You—Are You Ready to Receive?

Then I heard the voice of the Lord saying,
"Whom shall I send? And who will go for
us?" And I said, "Here am I. Send me!"

Isaiah 6:8

What are you waiting on? Sometimes it's imperative that we wait on the Lord—for answers to prayer, for confirmation to prayer, and so on. But many times, he is waiting on us! There's an old saying, "If you make one step, God will make two." God is waiting for you to make the first move—and then you'll be doubly blessed!

In 1995, I took a buyout from the newspaper I worked for. My job wasn't up for elimination, thank God, but I figured it was a good time to step out in faith and pursue my writing career. Even though I was a project manager when I left the paper, I never gave up my love for copywriting. So I decided to build my books of clients (I had zero). I started to think about the companies I'd *like* to write for and made a list. I sent résumés, wrote cover letters, and followed up. I had a decent portfolio and shopped it around to the executives on my list. By the end of three months, I'd secured freelance work with a major publishing house, a national African American women's magazine, and a nationwide newspaper.

"Who hooked you up with those clients?" a copywriter friend wanted to know.

"No one," I replied. "I just knocked on doors."

And I did. I did everything I was supposed to do—researched companies, sent out résumés, took meetings, presented my work—and God did the rest. I did my part (faith plus works), and he did his (blessings). The point is, *you* have to do something; you can't push it all off on God. He's not *waiting* to bless you—he's *ready* to bless you now!

POWER MOVE

What are you waiting on God for—answers, confirmation, action? While you wait, do. Think about a movie set. When the director yells, "Action!" the script that was written comes to life. The actors transform themselves, and everything changes. So it is with God. When we take action, that's the Lord's cue to move on our behalf. Take out your paper or journal—wherever you've written down your dreams and goals. What needs to happen to make them a reality? If it's within your power, make the next move today.

MY CONFESSION

I will step out in faith today, knowing the Lord is waiting to guide me.

72

Get in the Mix

Polish Your Networking Skills

Let us consider how we may spur one
another on toward love and good deeds.

Hebrews 10:24

Networking is essential to any career or profession. *People* hire people. *People* interview people. The human interaction is inevitable. You can join trade organizations, support groups, or social networking sites to meet like-minded people and learn about job leads and industry news. The more people who know that you want to get into a particular field, the better your chances will be of getting into that industry. And the more knowledge you can have about an industry or profession, especially one that is unknown to you, the better prepared you will be and the better your chances of getting the job or being promoted.

When I was freelancing after I left the newspaper I'd worked at for eight years, I did a ton of networking. I loved writing and wanted to shore up a few freelance gigs to supplement my dwindling severance payout. I met a young man at a Black Filmmaker Foundation meeting who said he had a friend who was a copywriter, so he'd put me in touch with him. His friend told me that the direct-mail company he worked for needed freelancers. I gave him my résumé and got hired almost on the spot. That freelance gig turned into a full-time job, which turned into a career that's still going strong after twelve years! Had I not put myself "in the mix" and made my intentions known, I may not have met my friend who introduced me to his friend at the company where I now work.

We tend to think of big events and programs when we think of making an impact, but Jesus knows the world changes only when people talk to each other. Take a lesson from Jesus, the master networker.

POWER MOVE

If you haven't joined a trade association in your area of interest, do so today. If you have, commit to going to the next meeting or gathering. Don't go with an agenda to meet a certain kind of person; be open to all kinds of connections. You never know what "angel" God has planted in the room to help you!

MY CONFESSION

I will make time to connect with others as Jesus did.

73

Get a Life

All Work and No Play Will Make You a Lonely Girl

By the seventh day God had finished the work he had been doing; so on the seventh day he rested from all his work.

Genesis 2:2

We're driven, we're successful, and we're ambitious. Like so many women, black women have been so achievement-oriented, we have forgotten to make time to have fun with our family, friends, or spouse. When we don't rest, our health suffers and our work suffers.

I never thought I'd be one of those work-obsessed, highly driven women who eat, drink, and sleep their job. But after I got my job in publishing, I discovered it was a whole new world for me: one with a built-in social life. The business lunches, lavish book parties, and publishing events provided experiences I never imagined a job would provide. My business life and my personal life intersected in many different ways.

I enjoyed my job and actually had fun at work. But on the weekends, I was so exhausted from the activity during the week that I found it hard to do the things I wanted to do—like visit with my family, plant my flowers, or just tool around in the shopping mall like other suburbanites. I became a slave to the job and its "perks." As a result, I became burned-out and irritable, acting out of character.

Right then and there I knew something had to change, so I did something I find so hard to do—I said no. I'm sure I wasn't missed at every book party, every luncheon, every networking event. They went on without me. So I didn't *need* to be there. After I revised and revamped my priorities, I spent more time with friends and family and started doing things I enjoyed. I became a happier wife, mother, sister, and friend. And ultimately a better employee.

POWER MOVE

You can be replaced on your job, but you cannot replace the time you spend with your grandmother, or your sister before she moves overseas. It's all about priorities. Even as you pursue your dreams, you can celebrate with the people in your life. Take a lesson from your success on the job, and schedule in time to play. Don't wait for a free moment on the calendar—make one!

MY CONFESSION

I will keep work, dreams, and goals in balance with the other good things God has given me.

74

Starting Out and Starting Over

Embrace New Beginnings

Behold, I will do a new thing; now it shall spring forth; shall ye not know it? I will even make a way in the wilderness, and rivers in the desert.

Isaiah 43:19 KJV

Beginnings can be intimidating. Think about the first time you went on a date. Your first day of college on a strange campus. The first day you brought your baby home from the hospital.

But beginnings can also be a time of great excitement and opportunity. Everyone's new start won't be the same. Some beginnings are rocky, and some are smooth as silk. Some new starts aren't by choice, though. With those, it's easy to hang on to bitterness and lost dreams, making it hard to move forward. And it's even worse when you compare yourself to others. Whether you're changing careers, returning to the workforce, or facing retirement, remember you're in a place God can use you. And admit to your own part in being where you are. Everyone has to start somewhere, but a new start doesn't have to be horrendous.

At age twenty-three, I'd just had my first son and was working at an ad agency as a receptionist. I was racked by self-doubt, kicking myself for not being where I thought I should be. I watched my friends work their way up the corporate ladder, getting promotion after promotion and big pay raises. Their salaries had surpassed mine—some were even double—as I stayed in the same job, struggling to pay the bills. But unlike them, I was a young, unwed mother practically straight out of college. There was no time for networking or putting in long hours to prove myself. I didn't have those freedoms. I had to get home to relieve my mother, who was with my infant son all day. I had chosen a different path once I decided to become a mother.

It seemed like everyone was doing their thing except me. I felt isolated and stuck. It was easy to think the Lord had forgotten about me because I didn't have the money or the advancement opportunities my friends had and made the huge mistake of comparing myself to them. I wasn't able to see the good in my situation as long as I was looking over my neighbor's fence. When I finally did look around, I realized I had a healthy son, a job with career possibilities, and a lot of support from my family. All those things were gifts, and I could consider each a fresh start.

POWER MOVE

First, look back. Take ownership for your part, good and bad, in your situation. Sometimes the hardships in our lives are a direct result of the choices we've made. Don't cry over spilled milk if you've made some mistakes. Turn the page and keep moving. Look forward to the new start you've been given. What are some great outcomes that could happen? Think about the possibilities and what you want your life to look like. Thank God for the chance of new beginnings.

MY CONFESSION

I will remember God is always doing something new in my life!

75

"I'm Only a ____________"

Don't Let Titles Limit You

Fear not, for I have redeemed you; I have summoned you by name; you are mine.

Isaiah 43:1

"I'm only a receptionist." "I'm only a telemarketer." "I'm only an administrative assistant." True, these are considered entry-level positions, but they don't define who you are. Insecure people may look down on you and think you're not ambitious because you are "only" a telemarketer. What they may not know is that although you may be a telemarketer by day, you're an incredible jazz background singer by night. You keep your day job in customer service for the steady paycheck and the benefits. You're one smart lady because you have the best of both worlds—titles and all.

I started out as a receptionist at a major ad agency right after college, but I had freelance writing gigs all along. When people would ask me why someone as cheery and intelligent as I was would want to be a receptionist, I'd say, "I'm actually a writer." I didn't identify with being a receptionist; I identified with being a writer because that's what I was. The receptionist gig paid the bills and provided health insurance for me and my infant son. It was a means to an end. But it wasn't who I was.

POWER MOVE

Many people were spreading vicious rumors about Jesus, calling him names and taunting him. Jesus asked Peter, "Who do you say I am?" (Matt. 16:15), and Peter gave the correct answer: "You are the Christ, the Son of the living God" (v. 16). Although Jesus became many things to Peter over the course of his ministry—teacher, friend, and confidante—Peter knew Jesus's true title. What's your dream title? Write it down. Now write down who you are—your character traits. Are you generous, optimistic, creative, honest? This is how to truly identify yourself. Workplace titles can change, but your character and personality are uniquely yours!

MY CONFESSION

I will not be defined by a title someone else gives me. I know my true identity comes from God.

76

Fearfully and Wonderfully Made

Celebrate Being a Daughter of the King

I will praise you because I am fearfully and wonderfully made; your works are wonderful, I know that full well.

PSALM 139:14

Black women are truly unique. When we commit our lives to Christ, he comes first in our lives, and our faith is the cornerstone of our being. When the Holy Spirit speaks to us, we praise him with the dance, without reservation or shame. If the pastor needs volunteers, we're the first to raise our hands. We make sure our hair is tight for Sunday service and the hat atop our heads is lying just right. We bring our special cultural "flava" to our surroundings, and that includes our workplace. For decades we've been at the lowest level of the socioeconomic totem pole. The media has vilified us by promoting stereotypes of either obese, nurturing mammies or loud-mouthed, hands-on-hips ghetto queens. Even though those negative images may have been forged in the minds of America, they were never our perceptions of ourselves. We are daughters of the king—the Most High God—and we should never forget that.

Although I had friends of all races and would lunch with them regularly, I always looked forward to meeting with the black women in our company for our monthly "sista lunch." It would be only about a dozen or so of us, but it was our chance to share stories, catch up with what was going on in our individual departments, and just have some good old girl talk. Many of us were in managerial positions and our jobs were stressful, so when we got around one another, we may have relaxed our work dialogue a bit or broken a verb or two. There was no pressure. We would get loud. We would say, "Girrrl!" and break into laughter over something silly. It felt good to have my monthly fix.

POWER MOVE

Sisters like First Lady Michelle Obama have given America a new view of what it means to be a smart, God-fearing, proud, and successful black woman. Think about ways you can give of yourself to another young sister who needs your help. If you fellowship with a group of black women at work, think of ways to empower each other, pray for each other, and encourage each other in the Word of God. Even if you don't all work in the same company, set aside time each month or quarter to meet. You are your sister's keeper!

MY CONFESSION

I thank God for my uniqueness as a black woman and celebrate that he made me for his glory.

77

Fridays and Mondays

Don't Abuse Sick Days

Whatever you do, whether in word or deed,
do it all in the name of the Lord Jesus, giving
thanks to God the Father through him.

Colossians 3:17

My friends in human resources tell me most people call in sick on Fridays and Mondays, which just happen to bookend the weekend. If your company pays for sick days, use them if you need to. But they're not an invitation to go to the beach or catch up on your shopping. That's what vacation and personal days are for. When you're out, someone else has to pick up the slack—be it another co-worker or a temp the company has hired to replace you. A sniffle or mild cold doesn't necessarily warrant a day in bed.

Employees who abuse sick days may ask their boss, "You don't want me to come to work sick, do you?" They shouldn't be surprised if their boss's answer is, "Actually, I do!" Don't wait for your boss to come back with that response. Instead, try never to ask the question. If you go to work and feel worse, you can always go home early.

Abusing sick days is like stealing from the company. Worse yet, it paints a negative picture of you. Your company's management may look not only at work performance but also at sick days and other criteria when doling out promotions, raises, and bonuses. They want to reward someone who is dependable, not someone who often seems to be out on Fridays and Mondays.

The higher someone moves up in their organization, the more imperative it is that they come in to work. When busy executives are out sick, it means missed meetings, lapsed deadlines, and unsupervised staff. So most executive-level employees work hard to stay healthy—exercising regularly, eating a proper diet, and managing their stress. They know the value of being at work every day.

POWER MOVE

Do you call in for every little thing? There's a difference between being sick and being sleepy. Take a look at your track record of sick days. Where can you improve? And if you are sick and will be out for an extended amount of time, have a doctor's note handy just in case your boss or human resources department asks for it. In a nutshell, try to stay healthy. Who wants to be sick anyway?

MY CONFESSION

I will honor God by doing what I was hired to do, on the days I was hired to do it.

78

All Change Is Not Bad

Embrace the Positives That Change Brings

Commit to the LORD whatever you do, and your plans will succeed.

PROVERBS 16:3

Change is inevitable. The seasons change. The weather changes. Our looks change. Relationships change. It's a basic process of life. Jesus even said that if we didn't change and become like little children, we'd never see the kingdom of heaven (Matt. 18:3). So things—and people—will not stay the same.

This is also true of work life. The boss you had for ten years decides to relocate for her husband's health, and you get a new boss. Your company has always closed early on Fridays in the summer, but not this year.

I remember when our company was merged with a sister company, and we learned we'd be moving to their new offices. I thought to myself, *Oh no, not again.* We had already moved twice and had "lived" in some of New York City's landmark neighborhoods—Times Square, Rockefeller Center, the Flatiron District. But little did I know God had the perfect location for me. When I learned that we'd be moving to Herald Square (home of the famous Macy's department store), I jumped for joy. The building itself was located directly above my commuter train station, so I could eliminate my subway fares and not have to pay additional commuting costs! I didn't even have to leave the building—I simply had to come upstairs to take the escalator, and I'd be in the lobby of my building. This shaved twenty minutes off my commute time, so the change, for me, was a blessing.

The people who adapt to change the easiest are the ones who will be the happiest. Do you resist change and see the negative, or do you embrace it and see the positive? All change isn't bad. Every change has a positive aspect and brings a new possibility. And no matter what does change, you can hold on to a God who doesn't.

POWER MOVE

Sometimes change works in your favor, and sometimes it doesn't. Rapid and repeated change is hard to embrace. And if we didn't ask for a certain change, it's even harder. But you can succeed in a changing environment with the right attitude. Find a helpful habit that works for you when you're confronted with change. Try taking a walk around the block or writing out your thoughts on the good and bad aspects of the change. Develop at least one tool to help you cope.

MY CONFESSION

I will hold tightly to the Lord, who does not change, and keep a loose hold on everything else.

79

Develop a Spirit of Excellence

Expect the Best from Yourself and Others

Then this Daniel was preferred above
the presidents and princes, because an
excellent spirit was in him; and the king
thought to set him over the whole realm.

DANIEL 6:3 KJV

People who are diligent, trustworthy, meticulous, caring, and look at what's best for everyone in a situation show the hallmarks of an excellent spirit. These are the people that get four- and five-star ratings on their reviews. They are committed to doing 100 percent every day. These folks stand head and shoulders above the rest, which is what God wants us to do.

How do you become a person like this? By being faithful in the small tasks as well as the large ones. By doing careful work even if no one is looking. By looking at the desired outcome of a project, not just your own part. By suggesting new ways to get things done, even when it's scary to speak up.

You've seen people with a spirit of excellence. They hold their heads high, they're alert and attentive to the needs of others, and they're receptive to new ideas. If a task needs to be done, they're the first ones standing at the ready, pen and paper in hand to get the specifics. If they're ordering a meal for the department, they make sure that the order is correct, there are enough utensils, and everyone is comfortable. They don't do just enough to get by. They go above and beyond what they're supposed to do, and they do it with a smile.

Ask the Lord to give you an excellent spirit, just as he did for Daniel.

POWER MOVE

Don't worry if people are jealous of your diligence. You may be called a "suck-up," a "brownnoser," or a "company woman" by the slackers. They secretly envy you and wish they were as thorough as you are. But don't be hard on yourself if a project or task falls through the cracks. Even the most buttoned-up sisters make mistakes. None of us is perfect, so don't hold yourself to an unrealistic standard. Excellence and perfection are two different things: the former is a by-product of the heart (spirit); the latter is a by-product of the head (ego). Ignore the haters and just do your best every day.

MY CONFESSION

I will strive for excellence in all I do.

80

All Working Mothers Are Managers

Use Your Job Skills to Keep Things Cool at Home

These commandments that I give you today are to be upon your hearts. Impress them on your children. Talk about them when you sit at home and when you walk along the road, when you lie down and when you get up.

Deuteronomy 6:6–7

To become better "mom-agers," we have to implement our job skills at home. Think about it—you've got all the skills you need to make for a more organized home as well as workplace.

- **Communicating.** This is perhaps the most important aspect of just about every facet of life—a business, a household, or a marriage. Regular communication with the kids will save you (and them) a lot of heartache and screaming matches. Does your son have soccer practice on Saturdays now instead of Tuesday nights? It's his responsibility to tell you if he wants a ride. Communication is essential to setting boundaries and managing expectations with your husband and kids.
- **Holding meetings.** Just like at work, hold monthly or weekly meetings to touch base with all family members

on issues involving school, extracurricular activities, and chores, or just to give family members a forum to air grievances and share good news. They can be more formalized if you'd like, complete with an agenda, or you can keep it loose and informal, with just mental notes. But you should keep the meeting on a schedule—for example, every Saturday night at six p.m. or every third Sunday after church. Kids like routine and order!

- **Setting deadlines.** By setting deadlines, you help your kids manage their time, chores, homework, and extracurricular activities. Some kids are natural procrastinators and need to have a deadline for everything. For example, if they want to go to the movies on Saturday night, their chores need to be completed by four o'clock that afternoon. In this way they have a time frame with which to complete their assignments.
- **Setting goals.** When kids set goals, it gives them a sense of responsibility and achievement when those goals are met. Whether it's helping them save enough allowance to buy an iPod or planning the family's vacation to the Grand Canyon next year, get the kids involved. This will be a practice that will carry over into their adult lives.

POWER MOVE

There are so many important skills you learn at work that you can employ at home. Only a handful is listed above. See which other skills can be applied to make your home life easier.

MY CONFESSION

I will ask God to help me as I create order at home.

81

Save for a Rainy Day

Get a Savings Plan—You Never Know What May Come Up

Dishonest money dwindles away, but he who gathers money little by little makes it grow.

Proverbs 13:11

It's okay to wear the latest fashions and step around town in the hottest shoes, but it's even better (and hotter!) to have a healthy bank account in case you lose your job or an emergency comes up. Life is full of surprises, and not all of them are good. It doesn't matter where you are on the economic food chain; everyone needs a savings plan. A 401(k) is a given if your job offers it, but try to keep a portion of your savings liquid so you can put your hands on it quickly.

When I first started working, my good friend Ellen told me about the company's 401(k) plan, explaining how beneficial it is. So immediately I signed up for it once I became eligible, after a year of working. I didn't make much money back then and was pretty much living paycheck to paycheck, but I managed to eke out the minimum 3 percent contribution from my paycheck. The best part is, I didn't miss it at all! I was trying to dig myself out of credit card debt, so I couldn't contribute much toward my savings account. But

I doubled the minimum payment on the cards to get out of debt faster, which ultimately improved my credit rating. I had less disposable income and lived on a strict budget with exact amounts for commuter costs, lunches, allowances for the kids, and, of course, bills. It was a tough time for me. The upside was, within three years, I was completely debt free. All that penny-pinching and budgeting had paid off. I had more disposable income and more money to save for family vacations and the things I enjoyed doing.

A word to the wise: don't abuse credit cards. If you don't have the money to pay for something, think twice before handing over your plastic. The Bible is full of verses about money—the pitfalls of loving it (Eccles. 5:10; Matt. 6:24), the importance of good stewardship, and the devastation it can cause if you covet it à la Judas Iscariot (Matt. 27:5). I believe God wants us to give generously but also to be wise stewards and make our money grow. God is all about increase, not decrease!

POWER MOVE

If you aren't saving anything, now is the time to start. There are a lot of great books and websites with ideas for finding ways to save. Find one that works, and then put that money aside on a regular basis. Saving regularly—even $50 a month—will get you farther than waiting for a windfall. If you're saving already, think about ways you can put even more cash aside. Rainy days may come, and a strong financial umbrella can weather the storm!

MY CONFESSION

All gifts, including money, come from God. I will honor God by being a good steward.

82

Keeping Peace at Home

Make Time for Your Mate

She watches over the affairs of her household
and does not eat the bread of idleness.

Proverbs 31:27

When you work full-time, it's inevitable that someone is going to get shortchanged. There are only so many hours in a day, and it's impossible to please everyone. But your first ministry is to your family, and if you're married, that includes your spouse. In most working families, it's easy for couples to get so tangled up in paying bills, fixing leaky pipes, going to Little League practice, and attending church that they forget about each other. This opens the door for the enemy to come in and have a field day. His MO is to divide and conquer, and lack of companionship (and intimacy) is a perfect breeding ground for marital discord.

We love our men, but let's face it—men need extra TLC. So it's imperative that we keep the lines of communication open and make time for each other. Earmark once a week or once a month as your date night. Get a sitter for the kids and enjoy a relaxing night out on the town.

When our boys were little, every Friday was our family night. No matter what, that was our day to spend together as a family. In the lean years, my husband and I would take the boys to Burger King or McDonald's (that was all we could afford) and then bowling or to the indoor games arcade (Skee ball was our favorite!). As our incomes grew, we took them to better restaurants. But as they became teenagers, they got social lives of their own and had other plans, so what had been family night quickly segued into date night for my husband and me—and it's been ten years and counting!

POWER MOVE

Remind yourself that you work to live, not live to work. You and your mate can build a life together, but it takes some time. Make sure there is one time per day or one day per week that your other half knows he can get your undivided attention. It doesn't have to be expensive. Pack a romantic picnic for two, pull out a board game, or challenge him to a friendly game of bid whist or spades (just hope he's not a sore loser!). The bottom line is, spend quality time together. You'll have each other long after the kids are out of the house.

MY CONFESSION

I will thank God for the gift of my mate.

83

An End May Be Just the Beginning

Layoffs and Letdowns Can Be a Hidden Blessing

Being confident of this very thing, that he which hath begun a good work in you will perform it until the day of Jesus Christ.

PHILIPPIANS 1:6 KJV

You've probably heard the saying, "When God closes a door, he opens a window." Although it may be true, you may not feel immediately comforted by this phrase if you've been given a pink slip. More than likely, you're hurt, confused, and angry, and you may not be in the mood or frame of mind to hear anything. But as the days pass and your feelings become less raw, you will have a chance to actually hear God speaking to you. His Word says, "Yet have I not seen the righteous forsaken, nor his seed begging bread" (Ps. 37:25 KJV).

If you're a woman of faith, you know that everything happens for a reason. God knew this day would happen in your life, and he knows you will get through it. He has bigger and better things in store for you if you're patient and have faith.

One of my dear friends and colleagues was let go in a huge sweep of layoffs at her company. She had been at the company many years and had built a fine career. As her coworkers embraced her in tears, she was not sad or woeful. She viewed the layoff as a challenge to pursue her side business full-time. Yes, she would miss the cushy salary with its perks. But she now had an opportunity to spend more time with her children and to make her own hours. For once in her life, *she* would determine her salary, her hours, and her days. She'd never had that much control over her life, and it felt good!

POWER MOVE

If you've been let go from your job, allow yourself a chance to grieve for what might have been—and then move on. It's always a little scary when your security blanket (even a perceived one) is pulled from you. But "faith is the substance of things hoped for, the evidence of things not seen" (Heb. 11:1 KJV). If God can part the Red Sea, he can certainly bless you with another job or opportunity. God is with you and is waiting for you to walk through the doors he is opening on your behalf.

MY CONFESSION

I will trust God at all times, even if I lose my job.

84

Name It, Claim It, Do It!

Put Action behind Your Words to See Results

As the body without the spirit is dead,
so faith without deeds is dead.

James 2:26

It's easy to pick out a lofty goal or ambition (the "name it" part), then profess that particular thing as fact (the "claim it" part). But the most difficult part is something rarely talked about—the action it takes to back up these claims and professions of faith (the "do it" part). Your words do have power, and saying something out loud releases spiritual power into the heavenly realm. But that's not all you have to do. You can say you're going to become a great salsa dancer, but if you never take a dance class or perfect your moves, you'll never be a great salsa dancer. Pastor A. R. Bernard, president and CEO of Christian Cultural Center in Brooklyn, New York, said it best in one of his Twitter posts: "You can name it and claim it, but you better do something to get it! Affirmation without discipline leads to delusion." God is in the blessing business, but you have to do your part. He's given you everything you need, so put some action behind those words.

I'd always wanted to write a book, even when I was a kid. I was a book nerd and never ran out of reading material, so quite naturally I gravitated toward the writing life. Little did I know that it would be decades before I even attempted to become an author. When my editor approached me to do this book, I was thrilled—and nervous. Where would I find the time? Would people buy it? Would the Lord be pleased? All of these questions swirled through my head after I responded that I would be honored to write the book. Then the *real* work began.

Let me first say I have more profound respect for authors than I've ever had in my life. For years I had read their works, promoted their works, and helped sell their works. Little did I know how difficult (and lonely) the writing process was. Coming in at night after a full day's work and sitting down at the keyboard was a challenge indeed. Sometimes I'd be up until three a.m. and still had to go to work the next day. And because this was to be a book to edify sisters in Christ, I felt doubly responsible and accountable. It was the hardest thing I've ever had to do. But God would not have given me this assignment if he knew I couldn't do it. I had faith, but I had to put action (and hard work) behind it. This book wouldn't write itself—I had to write it.

POWER MOVE

Whether we spend our time doing or wishing, the days and weeks and years will pass. Time waits for no one. To see your dreams come true during the time God has allowed you, you're going to have to take action. What do you want to happen in the next year? The next five years? Name it, claim it—then do it!

MY CONFESSION

I will thank God for the dreams he's given me and the ability to achieve them.

85

Lord, I Need a Miracle!

When Things Look Hopeless, God Shows Up and Shows Out!

The righteous cry out, and the LORD hears them; he delivers them from all their troubles.

PSALM 34:17

When we think our situation is hopeless, that's when God shows out! How many of us have been to the brink of hopelessness, thinking that God had forgotten about us because we couldn't see a solution? The Bible says we live by faith and not by sight (2 Cor. 5:7), but when water starts to fill the boat, we panic. That's the time to hold faster to our faith, to pray, and to believe that God will deliver us from our seemingly hopeless situation.

When I became pregnant with my oldest son at age twenty-two, I didn't know what I would do. I was not married to my husband at the time, and he was in his last year of college. I was a receptionist at an ad agency and made very little money. Now I'd have not only myself to support but a child as well. And I hadn't bought as much as an undershirt for the baby, even though he was due in a few weeks.

Out of my seemingly hopeless circumstances, something miraculous happened: I accepted Christ as my Lord and Savior when I was eight months pregnant. As I recited the sinner's prayer, I knew an inner change had occurred. I'd never felt so sure of anything in my life. My problems and issues didn't change in those precious minutes, but my soul had. I had too much joy to wallow in self-pity. I was alive, reborn in the Spirit, and about to bring another life into this world. Little did I know this was just the beginning of an outpouring of God's abundance and blessing on my life.

Days before I was to go on maternity leave, my co-workers threw a huge baby shower for me with everything you can imagine a baby would need—three huge shopping bags of clothing, toiletries, a snowsuit from Bergdorf Goodman, Italian knit blankets, and a check for over $300. And the icing on the cake was the ride home from midtown to my Bronx apartment in a chauffeured stretch limo! I was awestruck the entire ride home.

Then two days later, my sorority sisters threw a baby shower for me, and I got another several hundred dollars' worth of clothes, swings, strollers—you name it. I got not only one baby shower but two. God always does exceedingly abundantly above all that we can ask or think (Eph. 3:20). God showed up and showed out! And all I did was believe.

POWER MOVE

Is there anything too hard for the Lord (Gen. 18:14)? What's causing you to lose hope today? Where do you need God to show up and show out? Place your need before him and ask for deliverance.

MY CONFESSION

I will walk by faith today and believe that God will deliver me, no matter how hopeless things look.

86

More Territory

Watch God Multiply Your Talents and Gifts

Jabez cried out to the God of Israel, "Oh, that you would bless me and enlarge my territory! Let your hand be with me."

1 CHRONICLES 4:10

If you are willing, God will multiply your gifts and talents to take you places you never thought you'd go. Who says you're on this earth to do one thing and one thing only? Think of all the singers who become actresses, the models who produce TV shows, the athletes who become successful businessmen. All of these famous folks started out doing one thing, and as they excelled in that area, other opportunities opened to them. God does the same with you—he enlarges your territory. As you excel in the position you have—whatever it may be—God will expand and multiply your talents if you ask him to.

My friend Byron Harmon was an executive producer at CBS News in New York City. He was well liked by his staff, conscientious, and fair, and he had a spirit of excellence about him that was undeniable. You could call Byron an overachiever—a strong work ethic was instilled in him by his late father, and he never forgot it. It followed him to the military, then on to several TV stations in smaller markets, and finally to CBS, where he won several Emmy Awards for excellence in broadcast news production.

A few years ago, CNN called Byron and asked him to be the senior executive producer of CNN International in Atlanta—a dream job for any news producer. Now he travels extensively across the globe, overseeing several hundred news reporters—and in first class at that! God stepped him up. Byron is also an author with a couple of novels under his belt, but his most inspirational book is his memoir, *God Gave Me Some Bad Advice*. Don't be misled by the humorous book title—Byron is a humble and committed Christian who credits God with all of his success.

POWER MOVE

Sometimes our opportunity for "more territory" comes because we simply say yes to the opportunity at hand. Many times we're so busy maximizing our efforts or worrying about synergy that we forget to let God lead—and that his ways are higher than ours. The next time you're asked if you want to try something new, just say yes, and see what God does.

MY CONFESSION

I will ask God for more ______________________ (fill in the blank).

87

Tough Decisions

What Would Jesus Do?

Let your conversation be always full of
grace, seasoned with salt, so that you
may know how to answer everyone.

COLOSSIANS 4:6

Confrontation is one of the hardest parts related to work, whether it's with someone you supervise or with a co-worker. And yet we move forward only when we move through the tough stuff on the job—and in life. Where would we be if our parents never confronted our bad behavior?

Personally, I'd rather do just about anything than confront someone. So when the need arises, I look to the Scriptures. Jesus somehow managed to confront people with the sin in their lives and yet leave them absolutely sure of his regard for them. He always separated the action from the person—good advice for all of us.

One of the hardest tasks I'd ever had to do was fire someone. My new hire was intelligent, personable, and had a lot of promise. But after three months, she still didn't "get it." Ours was a complex business, and employees needed certain skills in order to succeed at the job. So after conferring with my colleague whom this woman also reported to, we decided to let her go. Days before I had to do it, my stomach was in knots, and I prayed for a spirit of peace and understanding when I delivered the news. I was calm and respectful, because I really did like this young lady. But business is business, and she wasn't meeting my needs. I told her the areas she needed to improve on in order to become successful in her next job, which I think was useful information for her. I wished her well, gave her a hug (I couldn't resist), and collected her work ID.

Firing someone is the worst thing a supervisor will ever have to do in their career because it's life altering. Someone who depended on their job to put food on the table can't depend on it anymore. But at the same time, a boss's responsibility is to make sure the office runs smoothly and efficiently. After they've been warned several times, those who fail to meet the requirements of the job or have performance issues must be fired.

Even with all the rationale to terminate someone's employment, there should still be a human factor to all of it. As Christian bosses, we should exhibit the respect and integrity of Christ. These are people, after all, not objects.

POWER MOVE

Whether you must let someone go or have a difficult conversation, first pray. Then look at and discuss only the action or inaction involved—not the person. Weigh in all the factors, document the person's shortcomings, and give them ample time to get their act together. The truth is, we don't really know what motivates people, so it's important to allow them to improve before moving them on. Sometimes personal issues can cause people to act out of character and their work to suffer. Don't assume you know why they did what they did. If they still do not improve, they must be let go.

MY CONFESSION

Thank you, Lord, for leading me as I lead others. I know you are with me even during the most difficult conversations.

88

Pursue Your Passion

Work at Your Dream While Working Your Nine to Five

This is the confidence we have in approaching God: that if we ask anything according to his will, he hears us. And if we know that he hears us—whatever we ask—we know that we have what we asked of him.

1 John 5:14–15

Do you want to be a video producer? A freelance photographer? A hairstylist? You don't have to be a starving artist while you pursue your passion, whatever it might be. Keep your day job, but put in the extra time, hours, and resources it takes to get to your ultimate goal. Do your job with excellence and integrity, and God will bless your new venture. Your employers are paying you to do a job, so do it well until you secure the position or career you ultimately want. Jesus himself was a carpenter by trade (Matt. 13:55), and I'm sure he was a good one! However, when his earthly ministry began, he put his hammer down.

Everyone has a dream job or some form of work that isn't necessarily work. It's something we'd do for free if we could.

Those of us who are blessed enough to have this type of job should consider it a gift from God (Eccles. 5:19).

Pursue your passion wholeheartedly. You can do this while keeping your day job, but it will take planning, dedication, and perseverance. If you have a family, pursuing your dream will be challenging since you'll need to spend so much extra time on your new venture. So make it a family affair—as you move toward your dream, involve your spouse or children. Want to open a restaurant? If your kids are older, ask them to go online and research suppliers. Give them all the info they need—keywords, locations, and so on—to do an accurate search. Ask your hubby to join you while picking out furniture or commercial appliances. Some businesses are still very sexist, and a man's presence may help you get a fair price. (This works with auto mechanics!) If you're single, ask your friends to help. More than likely, they have connections that could be valuable to you. Just as it takes a village to raise a child, it takes a village to raise up successful entrepreneurs!

POWER MOVE

The best way to keep moving forward on your plan is to schedule time to work on it, just like your day job. Plan to spend three nights a week, one hour a day—whatever works best for you and your schedule. But make sure to plan downtime as well—you don't want to burn out. Some of your best ideas will come when you're just relaxing.

MY CONFESSION

I will ask for help from God and others for my dreams.

89

How to Love the Job You Hate

Other Things May Not Change, So You Have To

All the days of the oppressed are wretched,
but the cheerful heart has a continual feast.

Proverbs 15:15

Some people hate their job and everything about it—the people, the duties, the location, everything. And let's face it—some jobs are worth hating! But what do you do in a down economy with limited prospects? You turn a negative situation into a positive one. Chances are, the job, your duties, its people, and the location will not change. So you have to—starting with your attitude.

The way you view problems will ultimately determine how you solve them. This is a case of calling things that are not as though they were (Rom. 4:17). If you dislike your boss, confess that he or she is a fair boss and a blessing. If you don't like your pay or hours, confess, "I thank God for my paycheck and the hours I'm able to work." Words have power, so tap into the power of positive confession.

Before long, you will notice others' attitudes have changed. When we change, people around us do too, and so does our environment. As Christians, we have the power to change the atmosphere where we work. That "bad" boss may let you go home early to get a jump start on the weekend. Another co-worker may want to trade hours with you since she's back in school. You never know what may happen—things can change. But change will have to begin with you.

One of my relatives was hired to teach a special education class in a very underprivileged school district. She knew what she was getting into—the principal had warned her of the personal issues the kids had and the lack of participation on the parents' part. But because these were black children, she felt an obligation to try to make a difference, and she wanted to. They were our kids, after all.

On the first day of school, she went in as a soldier, armed with the Word and ready for battle. As she expected, most of the kids were unruly and disrespectful, but some of them were ready to learn and cooperative. And she was ready to teach. But she could see she'd have to take action in order to see results. So she came in early the next morning with a bottle of holy oil and prayed and anointed each seat in the classroom. When the kids came in later in the morning, she noticed they weren't as unruly as they had been. The trouble-makers were quieter than usual. She had to make changes in herself in order to change her environment. By the end of the school year, the kids loved her. She had turned a job she hated into a job she could love.

POWER MOVE

You have the power to change your environment. Jesus changed the atmosphere and the environment of every place he ministered. We have that same power in us. But it's up to us to exercise that resurrection power to bring new life to bad (or dead) situations.

MY CONFESSION

I thank God that his resurrection power can turn a bad situation into a blessing!

90

The Lord Giveth and the Lord Taketh Away

Remain Humble as You Achieve Success

Humility and fear of the Lord bring
wealth and honor and life.

Proverbs 22:4

When we've reached a certain point in our career or on our job—accolades, awards, commendations, promotions, and so on—it's easy to start thinking of ourselves more highly than we ought to (Rom. 12:3). It's great to have accomplished so much—we're a success! And it's wonderful when success comes with perks. But we aren't entitled to those extras, and we don't need to get a reputation as a diva. The Bible says, "When pride comes, then comes disgrace, but with humility comes wisdom" (Prov. 11:2). So it pays to be thankful and humble. The things the Lord has blessed us with he can easily take away if he sees we could be destroyed by them. He loves us that much.

As the editor-in-chief of the country's largest African American book club, I've experienced things I never thought

I would in a lifetime. I've dined with power players, seen different parts of the world, spoken to various audiences, and visited celebrities' homes. Just ten years prior, I was a bored copywriter, looking for a new career path. I had no idea where that job would lead me.

At the time, our parent company was an international media conglomerate and held its annual conference for its executives in Berlin, Germany. I had secured one of my authors to attend this event and represent the book clubs, but secretly wished I could go. I had never been to Europe but had heard great things about it. *Lord,* I prayed, *I'd really like to go on this trip.* Employees on my level were not invited to go—only senior VPs and above. Plus, the trip was expensive, so I knew it would be a long shot. But the next week, I got invited to go by our CEO! I could barely contain my excitement (I think I screamed!). Although I would officially be escorting my author and her spouse, I still got to attend the meetings and see the city.

I remember an especially poignant moment while there. We were at a luncheon in a building that overlooked all of downtown Berlin, and I stood at the floor-to-ceiling window and silently thanked God. I couldn't believe I was in this beautiful European city with some of the most powerful media minds in the world. Tears welled up in my eyes at the mere thought of how much God loved me and had granted me the desires of my heart. I'll never forget that moment or that day.

Let's not take any of God's blessings for granted. If we're not careful, we'll start believing our own hype. And that's when we fall into dangerous territory. "Pride goes before destruction, a haughty spirit before a fall" (Prov. 16:18). So be thankful, prayerful, and humble in your rise to the top.

POWER MOVE

Someone once said, "It's nice to be nice," and it really is. When you smile and say "thank you" and "please," you show the world that you are Christ's representative first and Miss Executive second. People remember when you're nice, and they won't forget when you're nasty. So always say "thank you," even if you're entitled to something, or even if other people are doing the job they're paid to do. Gratitude keeps us mindful that all gifts are from God.

MY CONFESSION

I will remember who God is—and be thankful as I become successful. Amen.

Carol M. Mackey is editor-in-chief of the award-winning Black Expressions Book Club, the largest African American book club in the nation. She has been named among the 50 Most Powerful African Americans in Publishing by *Black Issues Book Review* and has been featured in *Literary Divas: The Top 100+ Most Admired African-American Women in Literature*. Widely recognized as a leading expert on African American book buyers, Mackey sits on the board for the National Book Club Conference. She has appeared on CBS-TV's morning news show in New York and is often interviewed by other media outlets on the state of African American publishing. She lives in New York with her family.